RHODE ISLAND
DISASTERS

RHODE ISLAND DISASTERS

TALES OF TRAGEDY BY AIR, SEA AND RAIL

JIM IGNASHER

Charleston | London

THE
History
PRESS

Published by The History Press
Charleston, SC 29403
www.historypress.net

Front and back cover photos courtesy of the *Woonsocket Call*.
Back cover pen-and-ink illustration by Bill Gallagher Jr.

First published 2010

Manufactured in the United States

ISBN 978.1.60949.100.0

Library of Congress Cataloging-in-Publication Data
Ignasher, Jim.
Rhode Island disasters : tales of tragedy by air, sea, and rail / Jim Ignasher ; illustrations
by Bill Gallagher, Jr.
p. cm.
Includes bibliographical references.
ISBN 978-1-60949-100-0
1. Rhode Island--History--19th century--Anecdotes. 2. Rhode Island--History--20th
century--Anecdotes. 3. Disasters--Rhode Island--History--19th century--Anecdotes. 4.
Disasters--Rhode Island--History--20th century--Anecdotes. 5. Rhode Island--History,
Local--Anecdotes. I. Title.

F79.6.I4 2010
974.5--dc22
2010043169

To my father and stepmother,
Anthony and Betsy Ignasher

CONTENTS

Contents

ACKNOWLEDGEMENTS

The author wishes to thank the following people for helping to make this project a reality:

Chief Mark Ellis, Potterville Fire Department, Scituate, Rhode Island

John Emin Jr., Smithfield, Rhode Island

Bill Gallagher Jr., artist and illustrator, Greenville, Rhode Island

Barry M. Mechanic, publisher, the *Woonsocket Call*, Woonsocket, Rhode Island

Lieutenant Robert J. Scearce Jr., USAF retired, and his wife, Fran, Portland, Oregon

Lawrence D. Webster, aviation archaeologist and historian, Charlestown, Rhode Island

Those workers at the Rhode Island State Archives, various city and town halls, public libraries and historical societies who helped me in my search for information.

INTRODUCTION

M YSTERY SHROUDS PLANE CRASH, FIRE." This provocative headline to a
1942 newspaper article was the genesis of this book. The article was
only four lines long and basically stated that two army fighter planes had
collided in midair over Scituate, Rhode Island. Intrigued, I wanted to learn
more, but the only follow-up article I found indicated that the army wasn't
releasing any information. It left me wondering, why?

I happened upon the article in 2003. Those with firsthand knowledge of
the crash were gone, and police and fire records from sixty years earlier were
nonexistent. It wasn't until I obtained the now declassified military crash
investigation report that I learned the full details of what happened. It then
occurred to me that there had to be other tantalizing stories like this one
that those interested in local history would like to read about, and further
research proved this to be the case.

Presented here are little-known and long-forgotten tales from Rhode
Island's past pertaining to shipwrecks, railroad accidents and aviation crashes.
Some are thought provoking; others heart wrenching; and still others have
an unsolved mystery attached to them.

It doesn't take long for an incident, no matter how horrific, to be forgotten
or eclipsed by something new. Over time, those with firsthand knowledge
fade away, leaving only yellowed newspaper articles and vague hearsay
accounts. Sometimes, even seasoned historians are unaware that such events

occurred in their locality. With that in mind, it is hoped that this book will serve as a way to remember these forgotten tales of local history and allow the reader to ponder some of the unanswered questions. Perhaps there is someone out there who will be able to shed new light on an old mystery.

THE SINKING OF THE SS *METIS*

1872

R hode Island's waters are littered with shipwrecks, and there is a story behind each of them. Some stories have been told and retold many times, making certain wrecks famous, while the tales of other wrecks faded into obscurity not long after the vessel slipped beneath the waves, never to be seen again. This is the story of one of those long-forgotten wrecks: the disaster that befell the steamship *Metis* just off the coast of Watch Hill, Rhode Island, in 1872, with a loss of roughly seventy lives.

Never heard of the *Metis*? Perhaps that's not surprising, for it went down at a time when shipwrecks were more or less commonplace. From the mid-1800s to the early twentieth century, several steamship companies plied their trade in and around Rhode Island waters. Ships of that era were largely constructed of wood and sailed without the benefit of GPS navigation, radar or onboard computer systems. The seas were crowded with vessels, and accidents were inevitable.

On the night of August 30, 1872, the two-hundred-foot *Metis*, under the command of Captain Charles L. Burton, was making its way up Long Island Sound toward Newport with approximately 155 souls aboard. (The actual number of passengers was never positively established.) The weather was rough, and many passengers had retired early to the relative comfort of their cabins. Some were seasick, while others slept soundly to the rise and fall of the ship. As the night wore on, the storm grew worse, and visibility was poor.

The final tally of those lost in the *Metis* sinking has never been accurately calculated. Image from 1800s advertisement, *Picturesque Rhode Island*.

Stormy conditions on the open water were not unusual, and with schedules to keep, most steamer captains chose to press on in such circumstances.

While the *Metis* bobbed and rocked in the water, a relatively smaller ship, the schooner *Nettie Cushing*, commanded by Emery D. Jameson, was sailing in the opposite direction with a cargo of lime. The schooner was sail driven and, therefore, less maneuverable than the steamer.

At 3:00 a.m., the schooner passed south of Beaver Tail Light in Jamestown, and shortly before 4:00 a.m., its skipper had Watch Hill Light in sight. It was there Jameson spied the *Metis* making its way up the coast. Exactly what happened next has always been in dispute. Captain Jameson claimed that he had steered clear of the *Metis* when at the last moment the steamer cut in front of him, while those aboard the *Metis* asserted that the schooner unexpectedly altered course and crashed into the steamer. In either case, a collision between the two ships was the result.

Just after the collision, Jameson said that he hailed the *Metis* for help but got no reply, as the steamer continued on without stopping. Captain Burton asserted that he looked for the other ship but claimed it had left the area.

The *Nettie Cushing* had suffered heavy damage to its bow, but Jameson determined that it was still seaworthy, so instead of taking to lifeboats, he gave orders to set course for New London, Connecticut.

Aboard the *Metis* it was a different story. At first it was believed that the damage was light, but it was soon discovered that the hull had been breached below the waterline and the ship was flooding rapidly. While crewmen went below to see what they could do about emergency repairs, Captain Burton ordered the helmsman to make a straight run for shore, hoping to beach the ship before it sank. The *Metis* covered nearly a mile before the water reached the engine room and extinguished the boiler fires, thereby killing all power to the ship.

The impact between the two ships had been relatively light, for there had been no thunderous sound of splintering wood or terrific jolt to indicate a collision. Many passengers in their cabins weren't even aware of what had taken place. Some later related that they first learned of the accident from other passengers and not from members of the crew.

With the *Metis* dead in the water and listing badly, Captain Burton gave the order to abandon ship. Some, including most of the crew, took to the few lifeboats, leaving many behind. To his credit, Captain Burton refused to leave the ship and did his best to calm those still aboard. As the ship sank lower in the water, he and the others climbed to the top deck, hoping to stall the inevitable. At this point, some leapt into the water, preferring to take their chances swimming for shore rather than be pulled down with the ship.

The *Metis* belonged to the Providence and New York Steam Ship Company and was a relatively new ship. Originally launched in 1864 as a freighter, it was converted to a passenger steamer in 1871. As such, the upper deck of the ship had been added later and was therefore not part of the original framework. As the lower portion of the *Metis* sank beneath the waves, the upper deck miraculously broke free and remained afloat, thus saving the lives of those still clinging to it. The deck flexed with the movements of the sea, thereby preventing it from breaking apart, and held together with its human cargo as the tide carried it toward shore. Both the living and the dead were carried ashore at Watch Hill, not far from the Ocean House Hotel. Survivors were brought to the hotel for medical attention, and hotel guests generously donated clothing to those in need, as many had left their cabins in various states of undress.

As word of the disaster spread, several boats were launched to search for more survivors, but more often than not their mission became one of recovery rather than rescue.

The schooner *A.B. Belden* recovered the bodies of a man and woman each wearing a life vest with the name *Metis* stenciled on it. In the man's pockets rescuers found personal papers and a stateroom key bearing the number 13 on it. The woman, however, carried no identification other than a ring with the initials "N.A." engraved inside. Hers is a particularly sad and vexing story.

On August 29, one day before the disaster, a man named George Howard married a woman with those same initials in Sharon Springs, New York, and they booked passage on the *Metis* to visit relatives in Pawtucket. After the collision, they donned clothing and life jackets and went on deck to await rescue, but they were swept overboard by a rogue wave. Tossed about in the sea, they became separated, and Howard never saw his bride again. Mr. Howard survived the sinking and went to view the recovered body, assuming it to be his wife. In his distraught state of mind, he identified the corpse as his bride and took her home to her parents in New York. It was only then that it was discovered that the body was not that of Mrs. Howard but of a woman who strongly resembled her and happened to have the same initials. In the meantime, it was learned that another man had been searching for the very person Mr. Howard had mistaken for his wife. Mr. Howard eventually found his wife in a temporary morgue, still wearing the same clothing he had last seen her in.

One tale of survival concerned the ordeal experienced by Mrs. George Remington of New York City, a strong-willed and resourceful woman. She was awakened by other passengers, who informed her of the accident and advised her to don a life jacket. She had some trouble putting the life jacket on, and when she asked a man for help, he refused. Once on deck, she found another man holding a cork mattress who told her that if she could find one like it, she could use it to stay afloat. After locating one, she jumped into the water with it and soon found herself surrounded by others who had jumped with nothing. They quickly overwhelmed the tiny mattress, forcing Mrs. Remington to abandon it and look for something else. All the while, she was being tossed by the sea and struck by pieces of wreckage that left her cut and bruised. Through sheer determination, she managed to swim to a large piece of wreckage and climb on. A man joined her, and together they held on as the sea carried them toward shore.

While clinging to their raft of sorts, a woman holding a baby swam to them and begged to be brought aboard. The man denied her, saying she would pull them off if they tried to help her on, but Mrs. Remington extended her hand to the woman and managed to pull her out of the water. Sadly, a wave washed over them and took the baby out of the woman's arms. The three survivors continued clinging to the wreckage for about two hours until they came close enough to the floating upper deck to be brought aboard.

Another woman who survived the initial sinking was seen clinging to a piece of flotsam. Witnesses along the beach saw her frantically waving for help, but there was little they could do until she reached shore. Just as she was within a few feet of salvation, a huge wave capsized her. When would-be rescuers pulled her from the water she was dead.

One survivor of the sinking wrote a letter to the *Woonsocket Patriot* publicly criticizing the crew for failing to assist passengers or relate information during the disaster. However, there is at least one account that contradicts this. It involves the story of a *Metis* crewman who jumped overboard holding a cork mattress. While in the water, he found a young boy who had nothing to keep

Many lives were saved when the upper deck of the *Metis* broke free and remained afloat as the ship went under. *Illustration by Bill Gallagher Jr.*

him afloat, so the sailor offered to share the mattress. After a while, the boy lapsed into unconsciousness, but the sailor held his head above water. When a rescue boat arrived, they offered to take the sailor aboard, but he refused until they took the boy first. The boy appeared to be dead, his face ashen, his eyes half closed and his mouth agape. The rescue men said they were there to save the living and not recover the dead, but the sailor argued vehemently until they agreed to his terms. Once the lad was hauled into the boat, he began showing faint signs of life, and he was later revived.

Throughout the following days, wreckage of the *Metis* littered the shore and became half buried in the shifting sands. There was no official attempt to recover or remove it except by souvenir hunters who combed the beaches looking for things to take. It was surmised that some of the dead might still lie buried mere inches from the surface of the sand, along with some of the ship's artifacts. Most of the recovered dead were taken to a hall in nearby Stonington, Connecticut. There, those searching for missing relatives, as well as curiosity seekers, walked past to view the unidentified bodies.

A board of inquiry was convened in Providence to investigate the accident, but after hearing days of testimony from all involved, little was learned about the actual cause of the collision. Each captain blamed the other and maintained that his vessel had the right of way according to maritime law.

One point of contention was exactly where each ship came into contact with the other, i.e., bow, amidships or aft or above or below the water line. Captain Burton put forth a theory that the *Metis* was struck below the waterline as it heeled over in the rough sea, which caused a delay in locating the damage. Others discounted this possibility, stating that the *Metis* would have crushed the schooner upon rolling back and sent it to the bottom.

In the weeks that followed, the sea begrudgedly gave up more dead. Bodies came ashore all along the New England coast and the north shore of Long Island. Some possibly remained entombed in the wreck itself or were carried out to sea and never found. The official tally was sixty-five dead, but it was believed that the actual number ran higher, as passenger records were incomplete.

In a tragic twist of irony, seventeen-year-old Frederick Kendricks had been traveling on the *Metis* with his father at the time of the accident. Frederick survived the sinking but drowned the following June in Georgiaville Pond in Smithfield.

The water where the *Metis* went down is 130 feet deep. It was decided that the only way to determine once and for all what actually happened would be to raise the ship. Although not impossible, resources available in 1872 would have made this a monumental and expensive undertaking. Therefore, it was never done. What remains of the *Metis* still lies at the bottom, mute testimony to one of Rhode Island's worst shipwrecks.

NINE SECONDS

1895

It could be said that there are two kinds of disasters: those that come with warning and those that happen suddenly. Yet even with the unexpected, there can be a small lag time—the moments between when the realization of what's coming sets in and the inevitable event takes place. A case in point is the horrible train wreck that occurred in Woonsocket, Rhode Island, on October 6, 1895, which killed three and injured several others. When the realization of doom set in, the crew of a speeding freight train had nine seconds to make a choice: jump and save themselves or stay with the train in the hopes of saving others. Some chose the latter.

It was called the "Boat Train" because it ran round-trip daily from the docks of Providence to Worcester, Massachusetts, and back, with only limited stops. Although primarily a freight train, it did carry passengers and was the fastest freight in the Worcester Division of the New York, New Haven & Hartford Rail Road (NY, NH & HRR).

On the morning of October 6, the train left Providence with a crew of seven. There were the engineer, Chester "Chet" Lawton, Conductor John Murphy, Fireman Albert Holden and four brakemen: Edward Fay, William Dyxbee, George Monroe and McCormack Heaney. All were married, lived in Providence and were longtime railroad veterans. At age fifty-five, Lawton was the second-oldest engineer on the line and had only recently come back to work after being sick for two months.

Monroe had been with the NY, NH & HRR for nearly forty years, starting his career as a water boy and working his way up to brakeman, a hazardous job that required agility and quick thinking as one rode the roof of the train. In the nineteenth century, a train's brakes were applied by turning wheels located on the roof at the end of each car. One false move or moment of inattention could mean one's life. Monroe was later promoted to conductor, a more desirable job, which generally took one out of the elements and into the relative safety and comfort of a passenger car. He later gave up the position, deciding he liked being a brakeman better.

Conductor Murphy knew his job well and was noted for his strict requirement that all brakemen aboard his train be at their posts on the roof at all times. This was a prudent policy, since one never knew when an emergency could arise.

Once the Boat Train left Worcester, it was scheduled to pass through Blackstone Junction, a freight and passenger station located in Blackstone, Massachusetts, literally just feet from the Rhode Island border. On the Rhode Island side of the line stood a semicircular brick building called an engine house or roundhouse, where train engines were stored or repaired. This building could only be reached when a train engine passed through three "switches" that allowed it to move from one track to another, and in order to do so, all three switches had to be "open."

Once it passed Blackstone Junction, the Boat Train was scheduled to stop at Woonsocket Station, where it was to pick up another freight car before proceeding to Providence. The train's average running speed was thirty to thirty-five miles per hour, which was considered fast for the day, and it was necessary to maintain those speeds to keep the schedule. It was because the train ran so fast that only experienced crews were assigned to it, and other train engineers were supposed to watch for it and give it the right of way.

The Boat Train was scheduled to leave Worcester at 3:15 p.m. and pass through Blackstone Junction at 4:05 p.m. However, for some unexplained reason, the departure was delayed, and it didn't arrive until 4:16 p.m. This delay played a part in what was to come, but it wasn't the only factor that led to disaster. A switch that should have been closed was opened, and the safety signal that should have warned the engineer that it was open was temporarily out of service. Therefore, as the Boat Train approached Blackstone Junction at nearly forty miles per hour trying to make up for lost time, Engineer Lawton had no idea that danger lay ahead.

As the Boat Train hauling eight freight cars and a caboose rounded the bend at the junction, the brakemen were at their posts, waiting for Lawton to

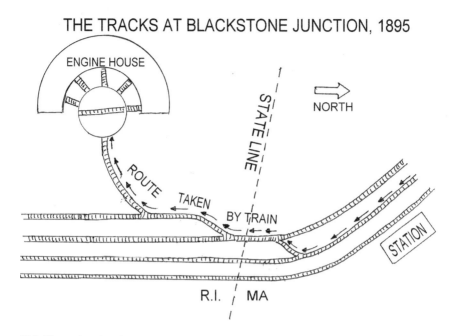

This illustration showing the route of the ill-fated Boat Train is based on a hand-drawn sketch that appeared in both the *Woonsocket Patriot* and the *Woonsocket Evening Reporter*.

give the toot of the whistle that would indicate it was time to begin applying the brakes so the train could slow down before reaching Woonsocket Station. Albert Holden was near the front of the train, followed at regular intervals by Edward Fay, William Dyxbee and George Monroe. Conductor Murphy and Brakeman Heaney were atop the caboose manning positions there.

As the train rolled through Blackstone Junction toward Providence, the locomotive ran into the first open switch that should have been closed. Almost immediately, Lawton blew the signal to apply the brakes. The brakemen went to work as fast as they could, for they, too, knew something was wrong since the train wasn't supposed to change tracks between Worcester and Providence—especially at that speed.

The train continued into Rhode Island and into a second open switch that put it on a course toward the engine house five hundred feet ahead. Lawton and the others knew from their vast collective experience that a wreck was inevitable, for a rolling freight train can take more than a mile to come to a stop. It was later calculated that a train traveling between thirty-five and forty miles per hour would cover five hundred feet in about nine seconds.

The crew of the train knew there was a good possibility that workers would be in the engine house, and as the train entered a third open switch leading directly into the engine house, each man had to decide for himself what to do next. No orders were shouted. There was no discussion. There wasn't time. Along the top of the train, some of the brakemen scrambled toward the rear, likely believing that they had tightened the brake wheels as much as they could, but there was no place to run. Others, like Edward Fay, remained at their posts.

In the cab of the engine, Lawton frantically worked the reverse throttle while sounding the whistle as a warning to those in the engine house. He knew that every mile per hour he could slow down the train could make the difference between life and death for everyone involved.

In front of the engine house was something called a turntable, which rotated over an open pit. It consisted of a length of track that could rotate 360 degrees so that train locomotives could be placed in individual stalls in the engine house. The length of track on top of the turntable was set perpendicular to the track the Boat Train was on. This observation confirmed to Lawton that the wreck was going to be bad.

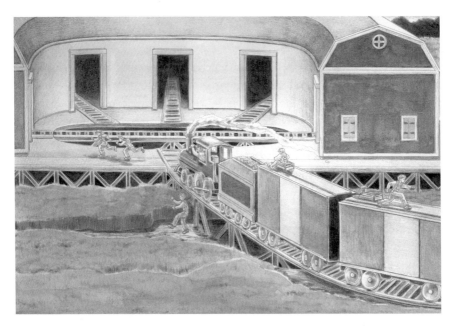

The crew of the Boat Train knew a horrific wreck was inevitable, and each man had to decide for himself what to do: jump to safety or remain at his post in the hope of saving others. *Illustration by Bill Gallagher Jr.*

In the final seconds, the train's wheels threw rooster-tail showers of sparks as they skidded along the rails; their metallic screech pierced the air and mixed with the long, high-pitched death scream of the steam whistle as the train moved toward oblivion and its crew toward eternity. There was a thunderous crash of metal as the engine struck the turntable, followed by the crashing and splintering sounds of the rest of the train's freight cars folding into one another like an accordion. When it was over, dust and steam from the wreck hung heavy in the afternoon air. As those in the rail yard began to recover from the initial shock of what they had witnessed, some ran to help and others went to notify authorities.

Lawton's warning had worked, for two men in the engine house had managed to flee just before the wreck. Unfortunately, Lawton was killed instantly, crushed and burned in the cab of his engine.

His fireman, Albert Holden, had jumped clear at the last second; there was nothing more he could have done. Holden was covered with wreckage and debris but was able to extricate himself, having suffered only minor injuries.

Of the five crewmen on top of the train, Brakeman Edward Fay was hurled forward and crushed between the telescoping freight cars. George Monroe suffered horrible burns from the escaping steam and died a painful death a few hours later. The others escaped injury due to skill, luck or both. Just before the crash, Brakeman William Dyxbee ran as fast as he could along the top of the train, leaping from one car to the next until he reached the caboose just as the engine hit the turntable pit. At that moment he threw himself flat and "rode down the crash." When it was over, he found himself on top of the pile of wreckage and simply climbed off. This was not the first train wreck Dyxbee had survived. Before coming to New England, he had worked for another railroad and had survived three previous train wrecks. Conductor Murphy and Brakeman Heaney were manning the brake wheel atop the caboose and were spared any injury when the caboose remained the only car not seriously damaged.

At the time of the wreck, there was one passenger aboard, an eighteen-year-old man who was tending to three prize racehorses being transported in one of the freight cars. The young man survived with minor injuries, but two of the horses did not.

As hundreds of spectators gathered at the scene, drawn by their curiosity, police from nearby jurisdictions had to be called in to help with crowd control. One man who failed to heed warnings to stay out of the way suffered a broken leg.

While rescue and recovery operations got underway, the question quickly turned to who was responsible for the open switch on the main line that set the disaster in motion. Some wondered if the act had been intentional and, if so, whether prosecution of those responsible could be hindered due to jurisdictional problems since the open switch was in Massachusetts and the deaths had occurred in Rhode Island.

Those who investigated the wreck interviewed surviving crew members of the ill-fated train, as well as the crew of another train that had left the area shortly before the accident. The investigation revealed that a conductor aboard the other train had absentmindedly left the first switch open after his train had passed through.

Railroad accidents in the nineteenth century were not uncommon, and safety for both railroad employees and passengers was of great concern. In 1893, the federal government instituted the Railroad Safety Appliance Act, which required, in part, that trains be equipped with braking systems that would allow the engineer to control the speed of the train without total reliance on brakemen. However, the act came with a grace period and was not slated to go into effect until 1898. The horrific wreck at Blackstone Junction was the worst to occur in Woonsocket, and newspaper reporters were quick to point out that such a braking system might have prevented this tragedy and warned the rail-traveling public that they all had a vested interest in railroad safety.

This accident has long since faded into history and from the public mind. The railroad tracks, the engine house and even the old train station that once composed Blackstone Junction are gone now, replaced by more modern development.

HIGH BALL!

1916

It's been said that there are two sides to every story and that the truth lies somewhere in between. Of course, this supposition is based on the premise that there is no absolute right or wrong, no black or white—just various shades of gray.

On the evening of April 18, 1916, an accident occurred on the New York, New Haven & Hartford Railroad that took the lives of five people and injured dozens of others. The cause of the wreck came down to a question concerning a railroad signal light. Some claimed it was showing "danger," while others maintained it was not. It seemed that there could be only one answer to the question, for there could be no in between; either the light was green or it was red. Who, then, was not telling the truth?

The tragedy began with two trains running late. The first was the No. 633, a local passenger train running between East Greenwich and New London. The 633 was making its way back toward Connecticut when it fell behind schedule due to a problem with the boiler. As the 633 passed through Wood River Junction, Engineer Donald Weatherbee decided he would stop at the tiny village of Bradford, located in Westerly near the Hopkinton town line. There he could effect repairs and transfer his passengers to another train.

Running about six minutes behind the local was the No. 25 train, known as the Gilt Edge Express. The express had left Boston earlier in the day and had been delayed twice along the way. Now it was chugging along at nearly

One of the casualties of the Bradford train wreck was a beautiful young woman trapped by debris. She begged for rescue as flames consumed the wreckage. *Illustration by Bill Gallagher Jr.*

fifty miles per hour to make up for lost time; this was permissible under railroad policy.

The engineers of both trains were unaware of the other's proximity, for under normal circumstances the 633 would have been well ahead of the No. 25.

A light fog covered the rails, but not enough to obscure visibility to the point where slower speeds were warranted. As the 633 pulled into Bradford Station, Weatherbee reported the boiler's condition to the stationmaster and was told to pull his train onto a siding in order to let the express pass by.

There seemed to be no great hurry to move the local from the main track to the siding, for it was believed that the red signal light indicating "danger" had been activated automatically when the 633 had passed. The light was designed to serve as a warning to any incoming trains that there was another train in the station. The signal would remain set at "danger" until the local pulled out of the station, triggering an automatic release switch. As a further precaution, a flagman walked several hundred feet up the tracks with a signal lantern to warn any train that might approach.

Meanwhile, the Gilt Edge Express bore down the tracks toward Bradford with Engineer Charles H. Mansfield at the helm and his fireman, Simon King, beside him. The express was hauling three passenger cars and one smoking car as it rumbled along in the fading light. As they approached Bradford, Mansfield saw a green signal light ahead, indicating it was safe to proceed, and called out "High ball!" to King, who rose from his seat to verify Mansfield's observation and called "High ball!" in return.

"High ball" was an old railroad term referring to a particular type of warning signal. In the early days of railroading, a colored ball would be run up a pole as a signal to indicate whether it was safe to proceed. In more modern times, electric colored lights replaced the balls. A green light meant it was safe, or "clear," to proceed; a yellow meant caution; and red signaled danger. If the engineer saw a green light, he would call out "High ball" to his fireman, who was supposed to verify that he, too, saw a green light and return the call. This procedure was done to ensure that both men agreed it was safe to proceed.

A few thousand feet down the tracks, the train would encounter another signal just before entering the station. As the express approached this signal, the crew saw that it was set to "danger" and, at the same time, saw the flagman frantically swinging his lantern. Beyond the flagman was the 633 still parked on the main tracks. Mansfield hit the air brakes, but he knew there wouldn't be enough time. The express plowed into the back of the 633 at about fifteen miles per hour, telescoping its locomotive into the rear car. The car had been illuminated with gas lighting, supplied by natural gas stored in a tank under the floor of the car. The tank ignited, and within seconds, the car was ablaze.

Witnesses later recalled how they saw a beautiful young woman pinned in the wreckage from the waist down, begging for rescue. As the flames and smoke swirled all around, roasting her alive, a man climbed into the inferno in a futile effort to free her. It was reported that he was so badly burned in the attempt that he would likely die from his injuries.

There was no fire department in Bradford, and by the time help arrived from Westerly Center, the train was completely engulfed in flames. Mansfield managed to save his train by backing it away from the inferno, thus averting a possible boiler explosion. Surprisingly, his train had suffered very little damage, and a few hours later it was allowed to continue to New London.

Incredibly, there were those aboard the express sitting in the smoking car who were totally unaware that an accident had occurred until they saw the glow of flames and realized a commotion was going on. One man, identified only as "Mr. Doheany," said that he and a companion had felt the collision but thought a coupling between the cars had come undone.

Dozens of passengers aboard the 633 were hurt. The more seriously injured were carried into the station's waiting room, but they soon had to be evacuated to a nearby post office when the burning train ignited the station. Before long, it, too, was consumed by the fire.

As the flames died down, all that remained of the 633 was a pile of glowing red embers and twisted steel. One man's body was so completely incinerated that only his torso was recovered. It was later identified by his wife from a fragment of clothing and a blackened pocket watch. An accounting showed five people dead, one missing and at least forty others injured.

No fewer than four separate investigations were begun into the incident. One was conducted by the Interstate Commerce Commission; another by the Public Utilities Commission; a third by the railroad; and yet another by Everett Kingsley, the coroner of Westerly. Coroner Kingsley's investigation was later taken over by the Rhode Island Attorney General's Office, which was permissible under state law.

Numerous witnesses were called to testify. The main focus of the investigation centered on the first warning switch; was it set to red or green? Engineer Mansfield and his fireman swore that the signal was green, but two other railroad employees who worked in the switch tower at Bradford testified that it was set to red.

Without going into long technical explanations of the workings of the signals, it was the general belief by everyone associated with the railroad that it was impossible for the first signal to have been showing a green light while the local was still in the station. Tests conducted by investigators seemed to bear this out, thereby pointing the finger of blame at the crew of the express.

Despite the long line of witnesses, the only two persons who could say they actually saw the color of the first signal light were Engineer Mansfield and his fireman. With no one to corroborate their story, some, including a grand jury, concluded they must be lying and recommended criminal charges, but only against Engineer Mansfield, since he was in charge of the train. A trial date was set for September.

In the meantime, what remained of the 633 train was buried on site in a trench dug alongside the tracks. There is one mystery connected to this accident, and it involves the disappearance of U.S. Army sergeant Carl Scott, who was believed to have been aboard the 633 at the time of the crash and since had not reported back for duty. It was rumored that his remains had been unintentionally buried with the wreckage, so on April 24, the trench was excavated. A few bones and pieces of clothing were all that was found, and the clothing was believed to belong to another victim. DNA testing did not exist in 1916, and with no conclusive proof that the bones belonged to the sergeant, the debris was reburied and the matter closed.

Engineer Mansfield had been with the railroad for more than thirty years and, by all accounts, had a good record. During the trial, Mansfield's attorney, Clarence Flaven, demonstrated that it was possible to manually manipulate the safety signal lights at Bradford by kicking a device known as a "gravity box," thus proving that the first light could have been showing green while the 633 was still in the station. He also brought forth other train engineers who testified to times when safety signals had been wrong in the past.

The trial lasted four weeks, making it the longest ever held in Washington County up to that time. The jury deliberated seven hours before returning a "not guilty" verdict. Cheers rose through the courtroom as the verdict was read, after which Mansfield was escorted to a victory banquet at a nearby hotel.

It would seem that Mansfield's acquittal adds credence to the old adage "the truth lies somewhere in between."

THE *CAPE FEAR* INCIDENT

1920

In one of the deepest portions of Narragansett Bay lies the long-forgotten shipwreck of the *Cape Fear*, sunk in a collision with the *City of Atlanta* on the evening of October 29, 1920. The reasons for this accident have never been fully explained.

The *Cape Fear* was part of the "Stone Fleet," a series of ships produced by the Liberty Shipbuilding Company of Wilmington, North Carolina, during and shortly after World War I. During the war, with materials such as steel and iron in short supply, an idea was put forth to construct ships with hulls made of concrete instead of iron. The idea was not a new one, for smaller boats had been constructed of concrete as early as the mid-1800s. It wasn't until the first oceangoing concrete ship was built in 1917 by N.K. Fougner of Norway that the idea really caught on.

The *Cape Fear* was less than a year old when it sailed from North Carolina to Providence in June 1920. There it lay at anchor throughout the summer and into autumn. On the afternoon of October 29, as it was getting ready to sail to Norfolk, Virginia, a shipping board clerical error led to two crews, one from Boston and the other from New York, showing up to man it. The *Cape Fear*'s skipper, Captain Harry Biggins, was forced to pay the wages of the Boston crewmen before sending them home, thereby taking on the crew from New York. The Boston men had no idea until later how lucky they actually were that day, for not only had they been paid for not working, but they had also escaped with their lives!

One would think that a ship constructed of concrete instead of iron would be nearly indestructible, yet it was not. *Illustration by Bill Gallagher Jr.*

At dusk, the *Cape Fear* steamed out of Providence and into Narragansett Bay. It was a clear night for sailing, and all seemed in order. At a point between Castle Hill and Rose Island, the ship encountered the passenger liner *City of Atlanta* under the command of Captain Bertram Garfield sailing in the opposite direction.

Captain Garfield later related that he had seen the running lights of the *Cape Fear* and had signaled with one blast of his ship's whistle, which was acknowledged with a single blast from the *Cape Fear* in return. Both ships, he said, had been bearing to the right of each other with plenty of room to safely pass when the *Cape Fear* inexplicably cut across the path of the *City of Atlanta*.

A ship is not like an automobile; it does not stop or maneuver quickly. Sometimes it can coast for more than a mile before responding to its helm. Captain Garfield ordered full reverse of the engines, but a collision was inevitable; the *City of Atlanta* struck the *Cape Fear* broadside, shattering the concrete hull as if it was porcelain. The sea gushed inward, sinking the *Cape Fear* within three minutes and sending nineteen crewmen to the bottom with it.

Rescue operations were begun immediately. Crewmen from the *City of Atlanta* threw rope lines to the sinking ship, but only five men from the *Cape Fear* managed to grab them. Others were forced into the chilly water, some sucked under as the ship went down. Of the thirty-four crewmen aboard the

Cape Fear, seventeen were saved, among them Captain Biggins, who suffered a severe scalp wound.

The *City of Atlanta* remained afloat despite heavy damage to its bow and later sailed into Providence under its own power. The Coast Guard searched the waters and shoreline looking for more survivors, but none was found.

Once repaired, the *City of Atlanta* continued service as a passenger liner, but it was an ill-fated ship. On February 10, 1925, it was involved in another collision with a barge in heavy fog off the coast of Baltimore. Five years later, it hit and sank the schooner *Azua* forty-seven miles off New Jersey.

During World War II, it served as a merchant cargo vessel, running needed supplies across the Atlantic for the war effort. On January 19, 1942, it met its fate when it was torpedoed and sunk in the Atlantic. Of the forty-seven brave men aboard, only three were saved.

The story of the *Cape Fear* has been forgotten with the passage of time, but its hull still lies on the bottom of Narragansett Bay in 125 feet of water, its concrete chambers serving as a stone mausoleum for anyone still aboard.

THE *MACKINAC* EXPLOSION

1925

It was August 18, 1925, and off-duty Woonsocket police captain Thomas O'Connor was enjoying the late afternoon sun on the top deck of the excursion steamer *Mackinac* as the vessel sailed out of Newport Harbor headed to Pawtucket. With him were three companions, also employees of the City of Woonsocket: Patrolmen John Flynn and Edward Howard, as well as Firefighter John Baggan.

It was shortly before 6:00 p.m., and the men were sitting comfortably on benches near the smokestack that protruded from the uppermost deck, but the stack was radiating heat, so they decided to move to the stern where a cooler breeze prevailed. O'Connor filled his tobacco pipe as the men made their way aft. Dance music could be heard seeping up from the decks below, where many of the 677 passengers aboard were being entertained. Just as the men reached the rear of the boat, O'Connor took out a match for his pipe, but before he could strike it, the ship's boiler exploded. Within seconds, the entire ship was enveloped in black soot and scalding steam. The music and laughter were now replaced with the desperate screams of those trapped below.

Captain O'Connor later related to reporters how he and the others "couldn't see two feet ahead" due to the thick steam and oily soot. True to their calling as men who routinely ran toward dangerous situations that others were trying to escape from, they blindly made their way forward,

Left: The explosion aboard the *Mackinac* left dozens horribly disfigured for life, but others were literally roasted alive. This advertisement, which appeared just three weeks before the explosion, casually mentions the ship's safety features, such as a steel hull and a wireless ship-to-shore communication system. *Author's collection.*

Below: True to their calling as public servants, Captain O'Connor and his companions helped to pull those trapped below to the relative safety of the upper decks. *Illustration by Bill Gallagher Jr.*

following the cries for help. On the decks below, deadly jets of scalding steam were shooting upward, filling the ship with vapors so hot that the skin of some victims literally fell away. Some passengers climbed out onto the gunwales in an effort to escape the holocaust; some clung to the ship, but others chose to jump overboard. A few of those who held fast to the gunwales were pulled to the relative safety of the upper deck by O'Connor and his companions.

The *Mackinac*'s commander, Captain George W. McVey, was in the wheelhouse with two ships officers when the explosion occurred, and he immediately ordered the transmission of an SOS. The ship was less than 100 yards off shore from the Newport Naval Training Station. Knowing that the ship had lost all power, he spun the wheel hard to the right and let its momentum carry it toward land, all the while sounding the ship's whistle to signal for help. The whistle was hardly needed, as the explosion had been witnessed by dozens of nearby private boats and U.S. naval vessels anchored in the bay. Many were already making preparations to rescue survivors from the water. Among those who participated in rescue efforts was Rhode Island Republican Senator Jesse H. Metcalf, who happened to be in the immediate vicinity with his personal boat when the disaster occurred.

The *Mackinac* came ashore, where it was immediately set upon by navy personnel who began tending to the wounded and the dead. Captain Charles E. Riggs, head physician at the base hospital, ordered all medical personnel and chaplains to the scene.

Pandemonium reigned as survivors were plucked from the waters while others were removed from the stricken ship. As word spread, police and fire apparatus streamed toward the scene. Newport Patrolman Tim Sullivan was one of those who responded. There, he encountered a ten-year-old girl with severely scalded arms who was in such pain that she asked the officer to blow on them.

Others arrived in delivery trucks and personal vehicles that were pressed into ambulance service to transport the injured. Women who had served as nurses during World War I came to volunteer their help. By midnight, the grim losses were tallied: thirty-two dead, four missing and forty-one others so badly burned that they were not expected to live. The question on everyone's minds was simple: how could such a thing have happened?

The *Mackinac* was a relatively new ship, built in 1909 at Ferrysburg, Michigan. It was 170 feet long and powered by two steam boilers. It was originally designed for freshwater travel and cruised the Great Lakes region until 1917, when it was acquired by the Blackstone Valley Transportation

Company and put into service on Narragansett Bay running day trips from Pawtucket to Providence, Newport and Oak Bluffs, Massachusetts.

The first hint of any trouble on the day of the disaster began before 10:00 a.m., when passengers arrived at the *Mackinac*'s dock along the Pawtucket River and were told they could not board right away, but no reason was given. As the passengers waited, workmen were seen boarding the boat and leaving a short while later. It was only then that passengers were allowed to board, and the *Mackinac* slipped its moorings and headed downriver, departure time delayed by forty-five minutes. It was this delay in getting underway that led investigators to first suspect that something was amiss.

The next clue came from a passenger who had once served in the British Merchant Marine tending boilers similar to those aboard the *Mackinac*. The man later told reporters that he had wandered down to the boiler room out of curiosity and had observed two crewmen working in four inches of water that was leaking from one of the boilers.

Based on this information, a criminal investigation was begun by Rhode Island's attorney general, Oscar Heltzen, to coincide with the federal investigation already underway by the United States Steamboat Inspection Service. Jurisdictional squabbles arose over the dual investigations, but it was finally decided by the U.S. district attorney that any criminal action related to the case fell under the purview of the State of Rhode Island.

Most of the passengers aboard the *Mackinac* were from Pawtucket and Central Falls, many being employees of a Pawtucket manufacturer that had sponsored the day trip for its workers. Others from Pawtucket included a group of fifteen Pawtucket police officers, some of whom were killed or injured in the disaster. One of those who died was Officer David Burns, who drowned when he jumped overboard to rescue a child struggling in the water. Another was Patrolman Henry Dickenson, who, although badly burned, refused medical help, stating that others needed it more. A third was Patrolman Elmer Whitaker, who, although seriously injured, tried to comfort and ease the suffering of others before succumbing to his injuries.

One retired Pawtucket officer aboard was John Harrison, who was blown into a bathroom along with three children when the explosion occurred. The room quickly filled with steam, and all were scalded. Though injured himself, he tried to keep the children cool by splashing water from the bowls on them and alternately holding their heads to an open porthole for air.

The force of the explosion yanked seven-week-old Bartholomew Wildenhain from his mother's arms. Fortunately, he suffered only minor injuries, but his mother died later of her burns.

There were hundreds of stories of sadness and escape to be told. Some potential passengers, frustrated by the *Mackinac*'s delay in leaving Pawtucket, had simply gone home, deciding to sail another day and thus saving their lives. One who had no choice but to sail was Ernest Hopkinson, a college student from Pawtucket, who had reported for duty to begin his first day as an oiler aboard the ship. He was killed when the explosion occurred. Another crewman who suffered fatal injuries was Brown University student John Hunter of Providence. He had taken a summer job aboard the *Mackinac* against his father's wishes. Yet another crewman who perished was twenty-one-year-old Frederick Lavallee, who had telephoned his mother from Newport saying he would be home that evening.

However, it wasn't just crewmen of the *Mackinac* who suffered; the civilian death toll was much worse. Five members of a Central Falls family were sitting below decks, with the mother nursing an infant daughter, when the blast occurred. Only the father survived.

Nineteen-year-old Martha McClelland of Pawtucket had been looking forward to the trip for weeks, having never been to Newport or aboard a ship before. She lost her fight for survival at the Newport Naval Hospital.

One badly injured woman wasn't told that her sister had perished in the hopes that she would have a better attitude toward recovery. She was released from the hospital after the funeral, and it was only then that she learned the truth.

Those who suffered the worst were below decks at the time of the explosion. Some, like Captain O'Connor and his friends, moved out of harm's way just before the blast, while others did just the opposite. A case in point concerned Annie Garceau and her two nieces, Delma and Helena Jauron, ages eleven and sixteen. They, along with friends and relatives, had been enjoying themselves on the *Mackinac*'s top deck when, shortly before the explosion, they went below to get a cold drink. Both girls were killed.

Two other girls were saved when their mother refused to let them go below for a drink for fear they would lose their seats. Instead, she gave them peaches to eat, which was what they were doing when the boiler exploded.

One who was supposed to have been on the ship but wasn't was South Attleboro Police Officer Charles Brogan, a friend of several of the Pawtucket officers on board. The night before, he had arrested a tramp and was forced to forgo the trip because he had to go to court.

It was estimated that had the ship been farther from land, or at its full capacity of one thousand passengers, the death toll would have been much higher.

Two who found themselves trapped below decks were eleven-year-old Harry Worthington and his friend Arthur Partington. Being resourceful and self-reliant lads, they managed to escape by climbing through a forward porthole and making their way to the ship's anchor, to which they clung until rescued. *Illustration by Bill Gallagher Jr.*

Those who escaped relatively uninjured were taken back to Pawtucket by a special train arranged for by Senator Metcalf. It was reported that the train was met by ten thousand people, some of them curious, but many clamoring to get news about friends and relatives.

The *Mackinac* was towed to Providence, where investigators found a twenty-six-inch split in one of the boilers, along with many pinholes and areas where the boiler's metal skin was extremely thin, all of which indicated severe deterioration in the unit. Records showed that the last inspection had been conducted in New York about four months earlier. Investigators wanted to determine when problems with the boiler first developed.

It was learned that employees of the Wholey Boiler Works had been summoned aboard the *Mackinac* on the morning of the disaster and that this had been the reason for the forty-five-minute delay in sailing. In sworn statements, Wholey employees said they were unable to repair a seven-inch crack in the boiler because to fix it properly, the boiler would have to be drained and lifted off the floor to gain access to the area that needed welding, and time did not permit such an undertaking. One employee testified that he had told the *Mackinac*'s chief engineer, John Grant, of the boiler's dangerous condition and alleged that Grant told him that if anything happened, he was to say it was a new crack.

As the investigation continued, the death toll continued to rise. In all, fifty-five people would lose their lives as a result of the failure to repair or replace a worn-out boiler. Others would bear the physical and emotional scars from that event for the rest of their lives.

Charges of negligence were filed by the United States Steamboat Inspection Service against Captain McVey, Chief Engineer Grant and Assistant Engineer George Mullen; however, the Inspection Service didn't have the authority to institute criminal penalties if the men were convicted. The worst it could do was revoke their navigation licenses, but the men could then file an appeal to have them reinstated.

At the hearing, testimony was given that the Wholey Boiler Works had been contracted to work on the *Mackinac* on previous occasions, but employees maintained that they hadn't done any work on the morning of the disaster. A representative of the Rhode Island Welding Company testified that his firm had been contacted on two previous occasions about doing repair work on the *Mackinac*, and each time the welder sent to do the job refused to make the repairs because the boilers lacked proper inspection certificates.

When Chief Engineer Grant was called to testify, he declined to answer any questions, despite the fact that he had done so on previous occasions. The judges took his refusal to cooperate as an admission of guilt and suspended his license.

Captain McVey testified that he had been in command of the *Mackinac* for five years and was unaware that the boilers were in a dangerous condition. He said he had seen welders aboard on the morning of the disaster but left the matter in the hands of Chief Engineer Grant.

The matter against Captain McVey was tabled for the time being because the judges wanted the chance to interview Assistant Engineer Mullen, who was still recovering in the hospital. They never got the chance to do so, for Mullen succumbed to his burns and died.

In October 1925, Rhode Island's attorney general brought criminal charges for manslaughter against Captain McVey and Chief Engineer Grant. George G. Kelley, general manager of the Blackstone Valley Transportation Company, which owned the *Mackinac*, was indicted and charged as an accessory before the fact. All pled not guilty, and the trial was set for May 1926.

Seven days into the trial, the defendants, acting on the advice of counsel, changed their pleas from "not guilty" to "NOLO," which essentially meant they were not admitting guilt but stipulated that there was most likely enough evidence to convict them. The change of pleas was accepted by the court,

The *Mackinac* monument, Tim Healy Way, Pawtucket. *Courtesy of the author.*

but only after closed deliberations by prosecutors and defense attorneys in the judge's chambers, the content of which was not revealed to the press.

However, Rhode Island's attorney general, Charles P. Sisson, refused to accept the plea agreement and ordered a new trial for the men. The second trial took place in April 1927, after which a jury found all three men innocent.

Any monetary compensation received by survivors or the families of those who died was pitiful, even by standards of the day. Peter McGuirk of Pawtucket lost his wife and three grandchildren in the disaster. When he received a check for $500, he promptly returned it, saying that others needed the money more then he did.

Surprisingly, despite the explosion, the *Mackinac* wasn't seriously damaged, and it returned to service as a freighter with the new name of *Woonsocket* in 1926. (There was already a steamer named *Pawtucket*.)

The people of Pawtucket have not forgotten the *Mackinac* disaster, for even today the repercussions of that long-ago blast still reverberate. In August 2000, seventy-five years after the incident, a monument honoring those who lost their lives was unveiled along the very section of the Pawtucket River where the *Mackinac* once sailed. Five survivors of the tragedy attended the ceremony, one of whom was Bart Wildenhain, who was torn from his mother's arms when the explosion occurred.

THE LEGACY OF THE S-51

1925

Volunteers Wanted: Must be willing to endure weeks or months confined in cramped quarters, breathing foul air, sleeping in a damp bed and seldom seeing sunshine. Work will be hazardous, pay will be low and if something goes wrong, one can be assured of a horrible death. Those interested can apply within.

Who would volunteer for a job like that? It may come as a surprise that many did. In fact, there were often waiting lists.

Those who serve in the United States Navy Submarine Service have always been an intrepid breed, and even today, one isn't forced to serve on a sub—he volunteers. A modern submarine is a technological marvel, spacious and well lit, with many safety features and amenities, but this wasn't always the case. The development of the submarine came at a terrible price.

The idea of the submarine had been around since the American Revolution, but it wasn't until the 1860s that the first true submarines were developed. Unfortunately, these early subs tended to submerge and stay down, trapping their crews in what some called "iron coffins." Mariners who found themselves in this predicament were totally on their own, since there was no way to call for help and there was no help to give.

By World War I, submarines had advanced to the point of semi-reliability, but crews who found themselves trapped on the ocean floor were still doomed to drown or suffocate, for deep-water rescue apparatus didn't exist.

Those lost in this terrible tragedy died a horrible death, but history proved that they didn't die in vain. *Illustration by Bill Gallagher Jr.*

The situation remained the same until a little-known disaster occurred off the coast of Rhode Island in 1925.

On the night of September 25, 1925, the passenger steamer *City of Rome* was making its way from New York to Boston southeast of Block Island when the captain saw a white light ahead riding low on the water and assumed it belonged to a rumrunner boat. The 1920s was the Prohibition era, a time when daring men made huge profits running illegal booze from ships to shore under the cover of night. The *City of Rome* was ablaze with lights, so the captain naturally assumed the rumrunner would take notice and steer clear, but he ordered a change in course as a precaution. This logic was sound, since most in the booze trade took special care not to be seen by anybody.

However, the light seen by the *City of Rome*'s captain was actually the mast light of the United States Navy Submarine S-51 on a patrol cruise out of New London, Connecticut. The men in the conning tower saw the steamship but assumed it would grant a military vessel the right of way.

As both vessels pressed forward, it soon became apparent that a collision was inevitable. Evasive action was taken, but it was too little, too late. The S-51 cut in front of the steamer and was struck just forward of the conning tower, tearing a huge gash in the submarine.

What occurred next happened quickly. Water began pouring into the S-51, and for many of the sailors inside there was nothing they could do to save themselves. The sub had been running under routine conditions and was not set for battle. Therefore, all internal watertight doors were open at the time of the collision. Those who might have managed to secure the watertight doors effectively entombed themselves inside.

Six men managed to escape through an engine room hatch, but three of them were pulled under by the suction created when the S-51 sank beneath them. The other three were brought aboard the steamship.

For those still aboard the S-51, their fate was sealed. One can only imagine the terror they felt as seawater shorted power from the electric batteries, leaving the sub in complete darkness as it plunged 125 feet to the bottom of the ocean.

Remarkably, the *City of Rome* had suffered only minor damage and radioed word of the accident to Boston. The navy destroyer *Putnam* was immediately dispatched to the area, where it found a makeshift buoy consisting of navy life vests floating on the surface, which indicated that some aboard the stricken sub might still be alive.

Rescue operations were begun, but options were limited due to the water's depth. The only way to reach the sub was by use of deep-sea divers, but the divers were limited in what they could do. The plan was to have two salvage cranes brought to the site and use them to raise the sub, but that would take time, and it was estimated that crewmen aboard the S-51 could only survive for about forty-eight hours before their air ran out or they succumbed to the bone-chilling cold. Unfortunately, a bad weather system moved in, stalling rescue efforts.

The S-51 had a crew complement of thirty-seven. Subtracting the six believed to have escaped the ship, it was assumed that thirty-one were still aboard.

Some good news was received when one crewman believed to have been aboard the S-51 was found safe at his father's home in New York. Seaman First Class Walter E. Harmon was supposed to sail with the rest of his crew but was granted special leave at the last minute because his father had become very ill. This discovery brought the number believed still aboard the S-51 down to thirty.

Choppy seas and bad weather kept the salvage cranes from their task until after the crucial forty-eight-hour time frame had passed. Afterward, divers reported that they no longer received any replies when they tapped on the outer hull of the sub.

The rescue mission now turned to one of recovery. Between stints of bad weather, divers bravely entered the sub and recovered eleven bodies. The first to be recovered were Engineman First Class John L. Gibson and Seaman First Class William C. Teschemacher. Nineteen-year-old Teschemacher had been serving aboard the S-51 with his twin brother, Frederick. More foul weather and a near-fatal accident to one of the divers put a halt to any further recovery operations.

The S-51 lay on the ocean floor until July 1926, when it was finally hauled to the surface supported by huge pontoons. It was planned that it be towed to the Brooklyn Naval Yard, where the rest of the crew could be removed, but misfortune followed when the S-51 ran aground on a reef while en route. It took twenty-four hours to free the sub.

The investigation into the accident revealed few clues. The steamship captain blamed the submarine, and the navy blamed the steamer. The debate dragged on, but in the end, it was decided that both vessels were at fault.

Blame aside, the sinking of the S-51 was used as a case study by the navy in the development of submarine rescue techniques. A rescue diving bell was later developed that could be attached to the watertight hatches of a downed submarine. In this way, trapped crewmen could be safely brought to the surface despite the depth of the water. Such a diving bell was used to rescue thirty-three crewmen trapped aboard another downed submarine, the USS *Squalus*, which sank in 245 feet of water off the coast of New Hampshire in May 1939. Such a rescue might not have been possible had it not been for the sinking of the S-51.

THE GREAT SWAMP WRECK

1926

There is a lonely stretch of railroad track in southern Rhode Island that runs for about three miles through the Great Swamp Wildlife Reservation. The land on either side of the tracks is considered sacred because in 1676 the final battle of King Philip's War took place there. In 1906, a monument to the incident was erected by the Rhode Island Society of Colonial Wars.

Railroad tracks once owned by the New York, New Haven & Hartford Railroad run less than a half mile south of the monument. They are still in use today, and virtually every passenger who travels this route does so totally unaware that there is another reason for the land to be sacred: a horrible railroad accident that occurred on this lonely section of track on June 25, 1926, that claimed the lives of four men.

It was about 3:30 a.m. on June 25 when a freight train hauling sixty cars passed the Kingston Station in South Kingstown. The train, bound from New Bedford to New London, was hauling heating oil, cotton cloth and American flags, which were destined for New York City's upcoming Fourth of July celebration.

The freight carried a crew of three: the engineer, William M. Roslindale, Fireman John J. Mulvaney and Brakeman George O. Hathaway. One can only imagine what was taking place aboard the train as it lumbered into the Great Swamp at twenty-five miles per hour, but this much is known: the

When the crew of one train vanished in the wink of an eye, there was nobody left to warn another train that disaster lay ahead. *Illustration by Bill Gallagher Jr.*

end was sudden, instantaneous and without warning. Perhaps the men were engaged in conversation, with one man's words cut short before a sentence could be completed. Maybe another had just poured himself some hot coffee from a thermos, and the end came as he brought the cup to his lips. A third may have been about to check the steam pressure gauges. If he did, and saw that the water was low and the pressure too high, there was nothing to be done, for it was already too late. All of this is pure speculation, for the end came as quickly as if someone had thrown a light switch; one second the men were here, and the next they weren't.

The sound of the freight locomotive exploding echoed across the swamp and was heard at Kingston Station about a mile and a half distant. Looking to the west toward the swamp, men at Kingston Station could see nothing but knew that something bad had happened. As they began making calls, they discovered that the situation was about to get worse. The wreck of the freight was bad enough, but the Cape Codder Express, bound from New York to Cape Cod, was racing toward the swamp from the opposite direction, and there was no way to warn it!

When the freight locomotive exploded, the blast blew a hole between the tracks 15 to 20 feet deep and hurled the boiler 135 feet into the swamp. Incredibly, the frame of the locomotive remained in place on the track, but the bodies of two of the crew were blown a considerable distance. Engineer Roslindale was found several freight-car lengths back covered and wrapped in bolt cloth. Brakeman Hathaway was found in the swamp 75 feet away with only his head above the water. The body of Fireman Mulvaney was never recovered, and it was assumed that he was either blown to bits or had been swallowed by the muck of the swamp.

Hundreds of American flags and bolts of cloth hung from nearby trees. Twelve oil tanker cars were torn open, spilling flammable heating oil across the area. Unfortunately, the oil did not ignite, for if it had, it would have warned the oncoming express. With the crew of the freight train all dead, there was nobody to even light a signal lantern.

It is estimated that the express came upon the scene within three minutes of the explosion. Engineer Chester Frazier and his fireman, Andrew Bennett, were in the cab of the Cape Codder as it entered the Great Swamp from Richmond. The time was about 3:37 a.m., it was still dark and the men didn't see what lay ahead until it was too late. The Cape Codder plowed into the wreckage and derailed, its locomotive ending up half submerged in the swamp. Both crewmen were seriously injured, Bennett fatally; however, most of the ninety-nine passengers aboard received only minor injuries.

State and federal investigators initially theorized that the explosion was the result of low water in the boiler, which led to overheating. Boiler explosions were a constant danger with steam locomotives. Therefore, it was imperative that train engineers maintain a constant watch on pressure gauges and water levels. However, veteran railroad men familiar with steam locomotives pointed to a weakness in the "crown sheet" of the boiler as the probable cause. They said it would have been impossible for the locomotive to have been able to haul the heavily laden freight train up the grade from Wickford Junction several miles away and then to the site of the explosion unless the engineer had topped off the water level beforehand. Therefore, it was concluded that a defect in the boiler was to blame.

Despite the loss of four lives in this accident, it could have been much worse had most of those aboard the express not been in sleeping berths.

There is no monument along the tracks to honor those lost in this tragedy, nor could it be seen if there was, for the area is remote and access along the tracks is forbidden. But if one stands quietly at the battle monument and listens carefully, he can hear the trains that still travel that lonesome stretch.

THE *BLACK DUCK* AFFAIR

1929

In 1922, the passage of the unpopular Volstead Act ushered in the Prohibition era, making alcohol consumption illegal in America. Almost immediately, bootleggers and rumrunners stepped forward to supply the wants of a liquor-thirsty public. Many deaths occurred as a result of the fierce and ruthless competition between liquor distributors, as well as encounters with law enforcement. A case in point happened on Narragansett Bay just off Newport on the night of December 29, 1929, and ended with three deaths. The incident, which some called a massacre, gained national attention and sparked several more violent encounters by self-appointed vigilantes. It all began when the Coast Guard attempted to stop a boat known as the *Black Duck*.

The forty-five-foot *Black Duck* was a notorious rumrunner based out of New Bedford, Massachusetts. It was faster than most Coast Guard boats of the day, which made it well suited for its job. On more than one occasion, attempts to catch it with a cargo of booze had failed, but that didn't stop its skipper from occasionally docking at the same piers utilized by the Coast Guard when empty. The rules of the game were simple: a rumrunner had to be caught in possession of the booze or there was no case. Whatever someone thought a rumrunner carried the day before didn't matter.

Rum boats generally rendezvoused with foreign ships anchored outside the three-mile limit of U.S. waters and, after taking on their cargo, made a

Though some called the Coast Guard's actions justifiable, others felt that what happened to the crew of a notorious rumrunner was nothing short of murder. *Illustration by Bill Gallagher Jr.*

straight run to shore, where the cargo was transferred to waiting trucks. The risks were high, but the money was good.

On the night in question, the *Black Duck* was slowly and quietly making its way toward Newport with five hundred cases of assorted liquor aboard. A low fog hung on the water, offering concealment, but the muffled puttering of the *Duck*'s motor was heard by the crew of the Coast Guard patrol boat 290, which navigated through the fog on an intercepting course. Cutting through the mist with a powerful searchlight, the coast guardsmen encountered the *Black Duck* just south of Dumpling Light and signaled it to stop by activating a siren. The *Black Duck*'s skipper immediately gave his engines full throttle in an attempt to get away, but the weight of the cargo slowed it down, allowing the patrol boat to keep up. There are differing accounts as to what happened next.

The Coast Guard maintained that as both craft sped across the water toward Newport, the 290 patrol boat fired a shell from its deck gun across the *Black Duck*'s bow as a warning to stop, but the rumrunner kept going. The cutter's searchlight revealed men scrambling about on the deck of the fleeing boat. In an attempt to disable the *Duck*'s engines, someone from the 290 opened up with a burst of machine-gun fire, reportedly aiming for the boat's stern, but at that exact moment, either the 290 crested a wave or the rumrunner chose that moment to take an evasive turn. In either case, twenty-one bullets peppered the wheelhouse, killing three men and wounding a fourth. None was found to be armed.

The sole survivor of the *Black Duck*'s crew was brought to Newport for arraignment and was released on $10,000 bail. It was there that he told a different account of what happened and asserted that the *Black Duck* was fired upon without warning. His allegations caught the attention of high-ranking political officials, who were quick to speak out against the shooting, which brought the incident into the national spotlight. One U.S. senator called for disarming the Coast Guard, as well as other federal agencies charged with liquor enforcement.

Others supported the Coast Guard's actions, citing law that allowed for shooting at rumrunners under certain circumstances; however, they wanted to know if warning shots had been fired first, as the law required.

One defender of the 290's crew was Admiral Frederick G. Billard, commander of the United States Coast Guard. The admiral made it clear that the Coast Guard had a job to do, and that job included the apprehension of smugglers of all types of contraband, including illicit booze.

As the Coast Guard and federal prosecutors began their investigations, Rhode Island's attorney general, Oscar L. Heltzen, began a state investigation, but he quickly discovered that federal authorities weren't being too forthcoming when it came to the exchange of information. He subpoenaed servicemen who were on medical duty at Fort Adams when the dead men were brought there by the Coast Guard. He also interviewed Newport's medical examiner, who had seen the bodies, and a newsman who testified that a Coast Guard officer had told him that the deck gun used to fire warning shots on the 290 had not been fired. General Heltzen was also able to examine the *Black Duck* for himself and determined that the pattern of bullet holes substantiated that the rumrunner was trying to get away at the time the Coast Guard had fired. He moved forward with convening a grand jury to press for manslaughter charges against the crew of the 290.

While the investigations were ongoing, it was reported that a drunken brawl took place in New London, Connecticut, that was said to involve members of the Coast Guard. Then, on January 4, 1930, members of the Moderation League held a demonstration denouncing the *Black Duck* shootings, calling the incident a "massacre in Newport Harbor." These two incidents helped to fuel the fires of public opinion against the Coast Guard. If news of the drunken brawl was true, then the Coast Guard looked like hypocrites, and the demonstration rally portrayed them as crazed killers.

Some were further outraged when Secretary of the Treasury Andrew Mellon came out in support of the 290's crew, stating that under current law they had acted properly.

On January 5, violence again erupted in New London when a group of vigilantes severely beat two coast guardsmen believing they were part of the 290's crew. They weren't. A Coast Guard captain blamed the attack on widespread publicity and statements made by "liquor smugglers, cheap politicians, and wet fanatics."

The *Black Duck* was brought from New London to Providence, where it was kept under guard by members of the Internal Revenue Service. Naturally, with all the publicity surrounding the event, curiosity seekers flocked to the pier hoping to get a look. On the same night of the attacks in New London, onlookers were threatened by the IRS agent guarding the boat. The agent, who was reportedly drunk, pointed two pistols at the crowd believing he was repelling "hijackers." As he waved the bystanders back, he fell face first on the ground, breaking a bottle of whiskey he had concealed in an inside pocket. He then stumbled to a telephone and called Boston asking for "reinforcements." When supervisory agents arrived, the guard was immediately suspended, but the incident served to escalate an already volatile situation.

The following day, a group of vigilantes attacked a houseboat belonging to a member of the 290's crew docked at New London. The crewman wasn't there, but his wife was. She was forced to cower in terror as the group broke several windows and caused other damage before police arrived.

On January 8, a letter to the editor appeared in the *New York Times* stating that officials who stood behind the actions of the 290's crew were missing the point. "The issue here is not whether force was justified," the author wrote, "but whether the particular kind of force employed was justified." The writer went on to state that the law of the sea allowed for a shot across the bow, through the rigging and then to the hull with the object of sinking the fleeing vessel, but humanity dictated rescuing the crew if possible. These sentiments echoed what many thought of the situation. It wasn't that the Coast Guard shot at the *Black Duck* to get it to stop; it was the fact that they had shot to kill.

A Rhode Island grand jury heard testimony from twenty-two witnesses, including the crewmen of the 290 and the sole survivor of the *Black Duck*, and concluded that there was insufficient evidence to indict on manslaughter charges. Likewise, federal investigators also found in favor of the crew, stating they had acted within the scope of the law. Coast Guard investigators also determined that the crew had followed proper operational procedure. Naturally, these findings were disappointing to some who had hoped the crew would serve time in prison.

Slightly more than a month later, a scene reminiscent of the *Black Duck* affair happened on February 26, 1930, when a Coast Guard cutter chased a suspected rumrunner from Newport Harbor to Fall River. After firing several shots from the cutter's deck gun, the rumrunner finally stopped, perhaps fearing that machine-gun fire would come next.

Another incident occurred the following July, when two men were wounded by machine-gun fire when they refused to stop for a Coast Guard boat off the coast of Falmouth, Massachusetts. It turned out they were not carrying any booze at the time. Surprisingly, neither of these two incidents sparked much controversy.

In another twist of irony, a federal judge ordered the *Black Duck* turned over to the Coast Guard for use as a patrol boat. Its quick speed, which was once an asset for outrunning the authorities, would now serve the Coast Guard in running down smugglers.

On August 26, 1930, the *Black Duck* captured a rumrunner off the coast of Prudence Island after a short chase in which one man was shot and wounded.

The former *Black Duck* continued to prowl the waters of Narragansett Bay until the end of Prohibition, searching for boats carrying the same illicit cargo that it had once carried.

There is a historic footnote to this story that's worth mentioning, and it comes to us from John T. Pierce Sr., author of *Historical Tracts of the Town of Portsmouth, Rhode Island*. In his book, Mr. Pierce relates that the secret to the *Black Duck's* amazing speed was the utilization of four high-powered aircraft engines instead of traditional marine engines. The navy later incorporated aircraft engines in the manufacture of its PT boats during World War II, an innovation that no doubt saved American lives and helped win the war.

THE JINXED AIRPLANE

1934

Can an airplane be jinxed? Some would say the one in this story was, for bad luck seemed to follow it everywhere it went. Others don't believe in such things. However, whether one calls it a jinx, a hex, a spell, a curse or simply bad luck, one thing is certain: the negative energy connected with this aircraft didn't end with its destruction.

The ill-fated aircraft was a World War I vintage Eaglebrook biplane, constructed of a wooden skeleton covered by a "doped" canvas skin. It was flimsy by today's standards and hopelessly obsolete even when it was still relatively new. It could transport a pilot and one passenger in two open cockpits set in tandem, each with flight controls so it could be flown from either the front or the back.

The plane originally belonged to a Providence man who had several accidents with it. On one occasion, he managed to tear the convertible roof off his automobile when he caught the plane's landing gear on it during what seemed like a perfect takeoff. Some might claim it was merely bad piloting skills, while others might say it was a harbinger of what was to come.

The owner eventually put the plane in storage at Montgomery Field, a small airport once located in North Smithfield, where it sat for several years until it was sold in 1933 to a Woonsocket man who repaired and repainted it. The Department of Commerce certified it as airworthy and issued a registration certificate, #NC5081. The registration was later suspended after yet another accident.

Was there a supernatural reason that hard luck seemed to follow a World War I vintage biplane, or was it all mere coincidence? *Courtesy of John Emin Jr.*

The new owner then fell into debt, and when he could no longer afford the hangar rent and storage fees, the plane was sold at auction, where it was bought by nineteen-year-old Ralph Wilkins of Slatersville for $150. Wilkins brought the plane to Woonsocket Airport, where he hoped to learn to fly. After some repairs, the plane's registration was reinstated.

When the original owner from Providence learned of the auction, he filed a lawsuit and obtained a court order for the plane to be returned to him. What claim he had to the aircraft is unclear, but after taking possession of it, he flew it to Hillsgrove Airport in Warwick and put it in storage there. Wilkins countersued and, after much legal wrangling, eventually won the case, but he incurred a certain amount of debt in the process. When the plane was returned to him, he had it brought to Smithfield Airport, which was located where Bryant University stands today.

While the lawsuit was working its way through the courts, Wilkins began taking flying lessons from Herman Dolbeck, a Woonsocket businessman who operated his own florist shop and was part owner of a corporation that sold personal airplanes. Dolbeck, a World War I veteran, owned his own airplane and was well known for flying over cemeteries on Memorial and Veteran's Day dropping flowers. He loved to fly, but his wife was fearful of his hobby and begged him to stop on more than one occasion. He had already survived one plane crash at What Cheer Airport in 1930, when the plane he was in hit some high-tension wires on takeoff and went down in a swamp. Although relatively unhurt from the ordeal, he later commented to a friend that someday he expected to be seriously injured or killed in a plane crash.

On the morning of May 28, 1934, Dolbeck met Wilkins at Smithfield Airport for flying lessons. They took off in Dolbeck's monoplane, and after a few hours, they landed at Woonsocket Airport, where the monoplane was routinely kept. The men then drove back to Smithfield Airport in Dolbeck's car and parked in front of the hangar where Wilkins kept his airplane.

It was now late in the afternoon, and the men hadn't planned to do any more flying that day, but just the same, they pulled Wilkins's plane out and started the engine while they waited for Ralph's father and brother to arrive to take him back to Slatersville. When they arrived, it happened Ralph's father had a camera, and he took several snapshots of the two men with the plane. After some brief discussion, Wilkins and Dolbeck changed their minds about more flying and decided to take the plane up for a quick test flight.

A mechanic who had been present would later testify that the engine sounded good to him, but a pilot who witnessed what came next stated that the plane appeared "loggy and heavy" as it gained altitude. Exactly what happened next was never conclusively determined. The engine had been warming up for over twenty minutes, and there was plenty of fuel in the tank. All that is known is that the plane managed to make half a circle around the airport before the motor sputtered and quit at an altitude of about 250 feet. The craft quickly lost altitude and crashed nose first to the ground. Dolbeck was killed instantly; Wilkins succumbed to his injuries a short time later. Since the plane was equipped with dual controls, it was never established who was flying it at the time of the crash.

Word of the accident spread quickly, and state troopers had to rope off the area to keep the dozens of spectators at bay. Investigators from the Department of Commerce learned that the plane did not have its original engine and the replacement was actually older than the aircraft itself. Therefore, engine failure was cited as the probable cause of the crash.

Dolbeck's funeral was held in Woonsocket with full military honors. Even though the "jinxed" plane had been destroyed, its pall of bad luck continued when a woman who was standing next to the casket conversing with a member of the honor guard suddenly collapsed and died of a heart attack.

On his way to St. Charles Cemetery and eternity, Dolbeck's hearse was accompanied by a flower truck adorned with a large airplane made of hundreds of flowers.

The wreckage of the ill-fated Eaglebrook was hauled away, the remains of which may still lie buried in some landfill or old dump. Can an airplane be jinxed? This particular one was involved in several accidents and one lawsuit, caused financial problems for its owners and was connected with three deaths. You decide.

A MYSTERIOUS MIDAIR COLLISION OVER SCITUATE

1942

October 30, 1942, was a beautiful autumn day, the kind that made one glad he lived in New England despite the fact that the country was in the midst of World War II. As the nation settled into "wartime mode," the populace got used to seeing the military prepare for overseas duty. So it was that two U.S. military fighter planes happened to be zooming through the sky over rural Scituate, Rhode Island, that afternoon.

The aircraft were P-40 Warhawks, planes already made famous by the American Volunteer Group, better known as the "Flying Tigers," who flew them in the China Burma India Campaign. The young pilots were putting the single-seat fighter planes through the paces, cutting across the sky making mock attack runs at each other. As one would attack, the other would evade.

The high-altitude "dogfight" attracted the attention of Mrs. Louise Ide, who was sitting at her post in a fire tower acting as a volunteer aircraft spotter. At least it was something to break up the long, lonely hours of her shift. As she looked on through her binoculars, she was shocked to see the two planes suddenly collide in midair. There was no explosion, just a quick smashing blow that sent pieces of one aircraft scattering across the sky that seemed to hang in suspension for a few moments as the other plane moved away. Ide's heart pounded as she watched in horror as one aircraft fell spinning out of control and then breathed a sigh of relief when she saw the white silk of a parachute billow open. The doomed airplane continued its downward plunge and slammed into the ground near Hunting House Road, where it exploded in a huge fireball.

The following day, one newspaper ran a cryptic headline: "Mystery Shrouds Plane Crash, Fire." The small article that followed was only four sentences long and basically said that the army wasn't releasing any information. Another newspaper ran an even smaller article, but it at least identified the pilots as Staff Sergeants John B. Robbins and John P. Palmer and went on to state that Palmer's plane was able to land safely.

There were no follow-up articles in either newspaper, and this was all the public was ever able to learn about the accident. That lack of information, coupled with the fact that officials weren't talking, suggested to some that there was more to the story, but with a war on, there was little time to wonder about such things. Mystery or not, with no fatalities involved, the incident was quickly forgotten and passed into history as nothing more than a footnote to the war.

Now, with the passage of time, the story of what happened can finally be told.

One question surrounding the event was the fact that both pilots were enlisted men, as Army Air Force pilots were generally commissioned officers. So how did two enlisted men come to be flying fighter planes? At the beginning of the war, the need for trained pilots was such that the army decided to reconsider its officer-pilot policy and allowed enlisted men who qualified to enter flight training.

According to the United States Air Force Museum, 2,576 enlisted men became pilots, graduating flight training as staff sergeants. Thus it was that 2 staff sergeants came to be piloting fighter planes over Scituate.

Declassified army investigation reports reveal that both pilots were part of the 325th Fighter Group, assigned to the 317th Fighter Squadron then based at Hillsgrove Air Field (today known as T.F. Green Airport). The 325th Fighter Group was established in New York on August 3, 1942, and transferred to Hillsgrove where the 317th, 318th and 319th Fighter Squadrons were assigned to it.

The group began with only twelve aircraft, all P-40s, which were older models that had been relegated to training status. With the delivery of these aircraft, operational training was begun, which included simulated aerial combat.

On October 13, the group suffered its first pilot fatality when Staff Sergeant Watkins Mayo lost control of his P-40 and crashed in Norwood, Massachusetts.

Seventeen days later, when Palmer and Robbins had their accident, they had been assigned to a ninety-minute training flight over western Rhode Island. After the collision, Robbins was forced to bail out but parachuted to safety. In his official statement to army investigators he recalled:

> *I was on a combat mission with S/Sgt Palmer who was flying Army 41-36495* [the plane's tail number]. *I was following him in a steep climbing turn to the left slight*[ly] *below him. When I realized I was too close to him I tried to break off to the right and down. He apparently stalled at the same time because he straightened his turn to keep from spinning and my left wing hit his fuselage at* [the] *root of* [the] *right wing. I only had enough control of my plane to fly to a wooded area and jump out.*

Sergeant Palmer's P-40 also suffered damage, but he managed to make it back to Hillsgrove and land safely. In his statement to investigators he related in part: "I was dog fighting [*sic*] with 40-498. We were turning to the left and my ship stalled. 40-498 was behind and slightly below. When he tried to break away to the right his left wing struck the fuselage of my plane."

A three-man accident investigation committee determined that part of the blame lay with the pilots and part lay with their commander for failing to assign a more experienced pilot to go along to supervise the training flight. This last part seems unfair to the commander, considering the lack of training aircraft available.

Noting that both pilots had received their flight ratings less than two months earlier, the investigation committee concluded in its report: "A memo will be sent to all squadrons requiring that all trainee pilots have their combat with older and more experienced pilots, until they have sufficient experience of their own." Exactly what would have turned out differently had a supervising pilot been along for the flight is not clear. There is no indication in the report that anyone was disciplined for their role in the collision.

A little more than two months after the accident, the 325th Fighter Group was transferred overseas and took part in many combat operations. Twenty-seven pilots of the 325th earned the coveted title of "Ace," meaning that they had shot down at least five enemy aircraft. Unit records show that Staff Sergeant John P. Palmer (later Lieutenant Palmer) was credited with shooting down three enemy planes in combat.

In November 1942, orders were issued for the promotion of all sergeant pilots to second lieutenants. Unfortunately, due to the rapid movement and redeployment of troops during the war, some promotion orders didn't catch up with some sergeant pilots until 1944. It is said that when some of these veteran pilots were promoted, they took their shiny new lieutenant's bars and scuffed them up so they would not be mistaken for rookie pilots.

This accident over Scituate was not unique, and literally hundreds more just like it would occur during the war, but in October 1942, with the war barely ten months old, the army had reason to want to keep such occurrences quiet. Pilots and air crews were volunteers, and the duty was hazardous—even during training.

IN THE SERVICE OF THEIR COUNTRY

1943

One may be surprised to learn that very little documentation exists pertaining to the two worst aviation disasters to ever occur on Rhode Island soil. In fact, even the most ardent historian might be hard-pressed to name them, for they weren't even recognized as such when they happened. Some may point to TWA Flight 800 and Egypt Air Flight 990 as the state's worst aviation accidents, or even to cases where military aircraft based in Rhode Island went down at sea, but none of these disasters happened on Rhode Island soil; only the investigations did. Therefore, in terms of loss of life, Rhode Island has seen two accidents that are tied as the state's worst aviation disasters, and both involved military aircraft at the Quonset Point Naval Air Station.

During World War II, Quonset Point played a vital role in coastal protection of the United States. Nazi subs were stalking Allied shipping convoys off our nation's coast with deadly results. In response to this, aircraft such as the U.S. Navy's PV-1 Ventura were assigned to anti-submarine duty. The Ventura was a twin-engine airplane that carried either bombs or depth charges to carry out search and destroy missions against enemy subs.

On the morning of December 5, 1943, a navy Ventura with six men aboard left Quonset to practice bombing techniques off Block Island. The crew consisted of the pilot, Lieutenant Walter P. Craig, radioman Max I. Colaw and crewmen Norman L. Simoneau, William G. Wheeler, Hugh Patrick Biddick and William E. O'Hern.

The plane returned to Quonset at 11:38 a.m., but during the landing, something went wrong. The aircraft suddenly careened out of control, smashed into Aviation Hangar #2 and exploded, killing all six crewmen and three servicemen working in the hangar: Luverne C. Kilinger, Walter E. Connelly and John S. Wojcik.

Despite the severity of this crash, there is surprisingly little documentation about it. The official navy report of the incident is brief:

> *Aircraft crossed edge of runway 34 at 50–75 ft. at approximately 100 knots. Plane made "buck of wheel" landing at too great a speed. Main wheels hit the ground first and then the tail-wheel, as the tail wheel hit—the plane bounced off the ground and assumed an unusual nose high altitude at which time the pilot pushed his engines full on in an apparent attempt to go around the field again. The main landing gear seemed to be retracting which would tend to verify that the pilot was attempting to go around again. The initial bounce plus the use of engines took the plane up to about 100 ft. of altitude in a very nose high attitude. Nose high tab used in landing probably increased the pilot's dilemma and ended with the plane in a full-power stall at 100 ft. The control surfaces in this stalled condition could not counter-act the torque at full power and the plane began a slow steady turn to the left barely maintaining altitude. When approximately 90 degrees to the original heading of 340 degrees, the plane's left wing began to slowly drop and at about the same time it struck the hangar and sheared off near the wing tip. The rest of the airplane crashed into the hangar and was consumed in flames.*

The resulting fire burned for twenty-five minutes until it was extinguished by base firefighters. One crewman from the plane managed to crawl out of the inferno but died the following day. Surprisingly, damage to the building was described as "slight."

News accounts of the tragedy were just as brief as the navy report, and there was no mention of it being the state's worst aviation accident to date at that time.

In more recent years, it had been suggested that Aviation Hangar #2 be preserved as a historic landmark; however, the building was demolished in 2010.

Seven years after the crash of the PV-1 Ventura, history repeated itself with another Quonset Point disaster in which nine more navy men lost their lives. That incident involved a navy P2V Neptune, a newer model of anti-submarine aircraft developed to replace the Ventura.

On June 1, 1950, a Neptune with a crew of eleven aboard was en route from Jacksonville, Florida, to Newfoundland when it stopped at Quonset Point for refueling. After the brief stopover, the plane continued on its way. Shortly after takeoff, a fire developed in one engine, forcing the pilot to return and make an emergency landing. On its final approach, the plane got caught in a cross wind, causing a crash landing on the runway, where it exploded into flames. The flames burned hot and fierce fed by the fully loaded fuel tanks. The pilot and co-pilot managed to escape through emergency hatches located above their seats, but the rest of the crew never had a chance and burned to death in the cramped quarters of the fuselage. Those lost in the accident were David M. Arter, Huilette E. Fountain, Francis J. McSwiggan, Clarence A. Payne, Clarence R. Plank, Peter Rapanick, John A. Seger, Harvey D. Thomas and Clarence A. Thorson.

Both of these aviation accidents remain the worst in terms of loss of life for the state of Rhode Island. It is hoped and prayed that they will never be surpassed. Although the servicemen lost in these disasters did not die in combat, they still gave their lives in the service of their country.

THUNDERBOLTS SWALLOWED BY FOG

1943

On February 11, 1943, a flight of four U.S. Army Air Force fighter planes known as P-47 Thunderbolts took off into the misty morning fog on what was to be a routine thirty-minute flight from Hillsgrove, Rhode Island, to Groton, Connecticut. None of them ever made it. Two planes crashed en route. A third is still officially missing (although its location is known), and the fourth flew off into oblivion and was never heard from again.

The ill-fated flight received brief coverage in the media, and within two days, with World War II in full swing, the incident became old news and moved out of the public eye. The results of the official army investigation were never made public. Not even the families of the lost pilots were privy to the reports. However, those once secret documents have now been declassified, and for the first time, the complete story of what happened that day can be told.

Weather at Hillsgrove was foggy that morning, with a low cloud ceiling beginning at nine hundred feet. Once airborne, the pilots would have no visual reference points to guide them, requiring them to rely on cockpit instruments such as the compass and artificial horizon to get them to Groton. Flying in such conditions is dangerous, for a pilot can lose his sense of equilibrium and not know up from down. In such circumstances the aircraft could be heading downward while the pilot believes it is flying level. Therefore, it is imperative that a pilot trust his instruments and not his senses.

The P-47 Thunderbolt was one of the best Allied fighter aircraft of World War II. It was big, fast, well armed and known for the massive amounts of battle damage it could absorb and still keep flying. *Courtesy of the National Museum of the U.S. Air Force, photo# 050616-F-1234P-009.*

The pilots were all young and relatively inexperienced. Only one had an instrument flight certification, but records indicate he had very little time at actual instrument flying. With the benefit of 20/20 hindsight, it's easy to say the flight should have been cancelled or at least postponed, but it wasn't. In fact, it appears that this wasn't even considered, even by the pilots about to make the trip.

The flight took off at 10:15 a.m. The flight leader was First Lieutenant Gene F. Drake. The other three pilots, all second lieutenants, were Raymond D. Burke, Robert F. Meyer and John Pavlovic. The men were assigned to the 21st Fighter Squadron of the 352nd Fighter Group, based at Trumbull Field in Groton.

Shortly after the planes became airborne, one of them seemed to disappear from formation, but before anyone could question what happened to it the remaining three left the area in a southerly direction and disappeared into the clouds.

The missing plane was piloted by Lieutenant Meyer, who likely lost sight of the others in the fog. It is surmised that with no visual references to guide him, he became disorientated and began heading north toward Cranston instead of southwest toward Groton. When he realized his mistake, he likely decided to drop down below the clouds to get a visual bearing on where he was. When he did, the wingtip of his aircraft clipped a stationary railroad car, and he crashed on the tracks just south of Park Avenue in Cranston. The plane exploded on impact, killing him instantly.

Meanwhile, the other three P-47s were apparently also lost, for they headed southeast toward Jamestown and Newport instead of toward Connecticut. While passing over Jamestown, Lieutenant Burke fell out of formation and crashed into the east passage of Narragansett Bay, while at about the same time, a third plane crashed into the water about five hundred yards off Fort Getty. The fourth plane was never heard from again.

Although training accidents were common during the war, it was highly unusual for an entire flight of four aircraft to be lost at once. An investigation committee was convened, and almost as soon as the investigation got underway the finger pointing began.

The committee consisted of three officers: a lieutenant colonel sent to Hillsgrove from Westover Field in Massachusetts; the lieutenant colonel in

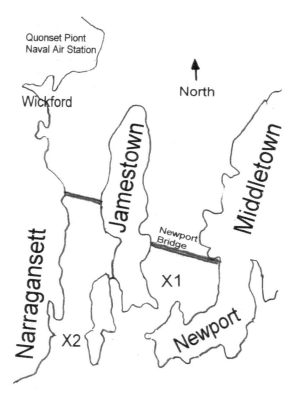

This map shows the locations of where two of the four P-47s crashed into Narragansett Bay. X1 indicates Lieutenant Burke's aircraft, and X2 indicates the other, unknown, aircraft. *Illustration by author.*

command of the 348th Fighter Group then stationed at Hillsgrove; and a captain serving as the Hillsgrove flight operations officer.

The investigation focused on who made the decision to allow the flight to take off under foggy conditions without the proper paperwork. Regulations required that the lead pilot, Lieutenant Drake, present his instrument certification card to the operations sergeant at the base operations office for flight approval. The sergeant later testified that Drake had told him his certification card was at Trumbull Field and gave the name of an officer who would grant the approval. The sergeant spoke with that officer on the phone and was advised to contact the captain in charge of Hillsgrove flight operations. According to the sergeant, the Hillsgrove operations captain authorized him over the phone to sign the flight clearance request without actually viewing the instrument certification card. However, the operations captain, who was also a member of the investigation committee, adamantly denied that he signed a clearance for Lieutenant Drake or that he authorized anyone else to do so.

Why the captain in charge of base flight operations was part of the investigation committee in this case is not clear, but apparently both he and the operations sergeant were later interviewed by Lieutenant Colonel Ora Young, the regional safety officer, who conducted an independent investigation.

A statement by the Hillsgrove flight operations captain taken on March 5, 1943, said in part: "Contrary to instructions given by me to the enlisted personnel at Base Operations that only contact clearances could be issued by the Clearance Clerk in my name, and that instrument clearances would have to be personally signed with my own signature, Sergeant —— signed my name to the clearance with his own initials under it."

When the operations sergeant was interviewed the following day, he said in part: "I Sergeant ——, then explained the complete situation to who I thought was Capt. ——, who gave me his permission to sign his name to the clearance of that flight of four P-47's, which is required."

Colonel Young stated in his report under "Comments": "It is the opinion of the R.S.O. [regional safety officer] making the investigation that one statement does not contain the truth and additional information received this date may verify this opinion."

Although Colonel Young did not specify in his report which of the two he believed to be telling the truth, he did state in part under "Final Conclusions," "The Operations Officer was not familiar with the weather and its trends other than local, therefore was not qualified to act in the capacity of an Operations Officer."

Under "Probable Cause" for the accident(s) he wrote: "Inexperienced personnel were approved for a flight involving instruments by an incompetent operations office."

While Colonel Young indicated that the operations office was to blame, the investigation committee reached a different conclusion and blamed the operations sergeant for signing the flight clearance allegedly without the knowledge of the operations officer, who, it was stated, was at a meeting when the flight took off. They further blamed Lieutenant Drake for initiating the flight without having his instrument certification card.

Of interest is the fact that one member of the investigation committee, the lieutenant colonel in command of the 348th Fighter group at Hillsgrove, did not sign the final report above his typewritten name. Why his signature is lacking can only be guessed at this late date, but perhaps he did not agree with the findings.

While the investigation was taking place at Hillsgrove, salvage operations had been underway off Jamestown. The body of Lieutenant Burke was recovered floating on the surface shortly after he crashed, but rough weather and floating ice prevented any recovery from the other plane that crashed off Fort Getty. Debris later found along the shoreline suggested that the aircraft might have broken up on impact, but this was not confirmed. If the plane broke apart, tides and currents would have carried the pilot's remains out to sea. Unfortunately, there is no mention in the report as to which of the two missing P-47s this wreck was believed to be.

Recovery efforts fell to the navy, as the army didn't have salvage boats, but the navy was busy with a salvage operation of its own in the same general area, searching for two navy planes and three missing men after a midair collision that occurred the day after the doomed P-47s left Hillsgrove. Then on February 22, a navy fighter went down off Block Island, and three days later a navy torpedo bomber went down over the Atlantic. Additionally, the P-47 at the bottom of Narragansett Bay was not the only army aircraft awaiting recovery. Records show that another P-47 had crashed elsewhere in the bay and another had gone down in the water on March 5 off Fishers Island near Groton. This is not to say one wreck was more important than another, but it illustrates the frequency of wartime aviation accidents.

On February 24, the navy turned the recovery matter back over to the army, stating that the salvage boat was needed in New York. As compensation, the army was offered the services of a mine layer based in Rhode Island, but the mine layer had its own mission priorities, which was the laying of anti-shipping mines.

There are no documents included with the investigation report to indicate that the third P-47 or the pilot were ever recovered. Circumstantial evidence points to the fact that the pilot of this aircraft had to be either Lieutenant Drake or Lieutenant Pavlovic. Research conducted at the Rhode Island State Archives, and at local cities and towns, failed to turn up death certificates for either of the two men, which indicates that their deaths, or even presumed deaths, were never reported to the state. A death certificate should have been filed if a recovery was made, and a presumption of death would normally have been filed one year after their disappearance.

Aside from the reasons already mentioned, the apparent lack of a recovery may have also been related to the fact that there was a war on with fast-breaking developments, rapidly changing priorities and the constant transfer of personnel in an era without computers. The colonel in charge of the accident investigation committee had only been detailed to Hillsgrove from Westover on a temporary basis until the investigation was complete. When he returned to Westover, he presumably left the final details in the hands of officials at Hillsgrove, but in April, the 348th Fighter Group at Hillsgrove was transferred to Westover.

However, the doomed flight of P-47s was part of the 352nd Fighter Group, which at that time was stationed at Trumbull Field in Groton, and nobody from the 352nd had been part of the investigation committee. At the time of the investigation, the 352nd was preparing to go overseas, and commanding officers there were dealing with several aircraft training accidents of their own. On February 16, a P-47 crash-landed at Trumbull airfield. Three days later, a P-47 from Trumbull Field crashed in Wakefield, Rhode Island. Four more Trumbull Field planes went down over the following two weeks. By early March, the 352nd had transferred to Mitchell Field on Long Island, New York. In effect, the recovery operation of the third P-47 was eclipsed by the war.

What happened to the fourth P-47 and its pilot will most likely never be known for certain, but presumably the pilot continued southeast out to sea, where he also met his fate. To this day, fishing boats dragging their nets along the floor of the Atlantic will occasionally snare a piece of World War II aircraft wreckage, but after so many years in salt water, virtually all means of positive identification have been lost.

Should they ever be found, the aircraft serial numbers to the two missing P-47s are as follows: Lieutenant Pavlovic, 41-5944; and Lieutenant Drake, 41-5922. Both are still out there—somewhere.

WILDCATS INTO THE WIND

1943

It was an unexpected late winter storm that lasted about twenty-four hours. It didn't drop much snow, but in its wake it left a mystery that has never been solved. Perhaps someone who reads this may provide the answer.

On March 30, 1943, the U.S. Navy aircraft carrier USS *Ranger* was just off the coast of Massachusetts steaming toward Boston for required maintenance. Wartime precautions dictated that the ship's aircraft complement be sent inland while the ship was in port in case of sabotage or enemy attack.

Below decks, the pilots joked in the ready room. Their destination was to be Rhode Island's Quonset Point Naval Air Station, a relatively short and routine flight. Some were looking forward to their stay in "Little Rhody," especially Lieutenant Arthur J. Cassidy Jr. of Cranston, Rhode Island, who eagerly wanted to be reunited with his new bride, Marie, whom he had married only four weeks earlier while home on leave. Many of the pilots, including Cassidy, were experienced combat veterans who had recently distinguished themselves in Operation Torch in North Africa.

That day, the National Weather Service in Boston predicted warmer weather toward evening, with no small craft or storm warnings along the Atlantic coast. Despite this prediction, a weather system was moving across upstate New York into New England, and cloud cover was spreading across the region. Therefore, the weather officer aboard the *Ranger* had written instructions on two blackboards in the pilot's ready room. On the first blackboard he had

During a snowstorm in 1943, a U.S. Navy Wildcat fighter similar to the one pictured here was last seen flying over land when it disappeared. The mystery of what happened to it has never been solved. *Courtesy of Department of the Navy—History & Heritage Command, photo # 80-G-224669.*

written, "Land at Squantum and obtain Quonset weather." The second board gave the navigational heading for Squantum Naval Air Station in Quincy, Massachusetts, just outside of Boston. According to the official navy investigation report (43-6393), for some unexplained reason, the pilots never saw the first blackboard, and apparently the briefing officer never informed the pilots that they were to fly to Squantum first. Therefore, upon leaving the *Ranger* the pilots headed straight for Quonset. This critical error led to disaster.

Once airborne, the planes became separated as bad weather blew in faster than expected, and each pilot was left to his own devices to find his way. Shortly after takeoff, one aircraft crash-landed in the water off the coast of Swampscott, Massachusetts, but the two-man crew was quickly rescued by the Coast Guard. Another *Ranger* plane crashed in Fall River, Massachusetts, but the pilot managed to bail out just in the nick of time. Three other aircraft in the flight got lost and ended up in the town of New Paltz, New York, where they made an emergency landing in an open field.

All but one of the remaining planes arrived safely at Quonset Point. After an accounting, it was learned that Lieutenant Cassidy and his aircraft, a Grumman Wildcat, were missing. There had been no other reports of downed aircraft, and it was hoped he had landed safely someplace to wait out the storm, but when he failed to report in, a search was quickly organized.

The search concentrated in the area of North Attleboro, Massachusetts, just over the Rhode Island state line, because a woman there reported seeing a navy plane in distress about 4:00 p.m. on the day of the storm. There is no proof that the plane she saw was actually Lieutenant Cassidy's, but it was accepted as such by the navy. This news led others to come forward claiming that they, too, had seen a navy plane in trouble, but no one could provide any useful information.

The search area was eventually widened to include several towns around North Attleboro and nearby northern Rhode Island, but despite the massive air and ground search, which included civilian volunteers, no trace of Lieutenant Cassidy or his airplane was ever found.

What happened to Lieutenant Cassidy remains open to speculation. One possibility is that his plane went down in a lake or a reservoir where it lies to this day with its pilot still strapped in his seat. There are numerous large bodies of water in the area that would be capable of swallowing a small airplane like a Wildcat.

It is also possible that, like others in the flight, he became lost and went down in a remote, wooded area or mountaintop. The falling snow could have muffled the sound of a crash, contained any fires and then covered what wreckage remained.

A third possibility is that he passed over Rhode Island and inadvertently flew out to sea, where he ran out of fuel and crashed.

The Wildcat was produced by Grumman Aircraft as a navy fighter plane for use on aircraft carriers. The serial number of Lieutenant Cassidy's plane was BuNo.11740, and his military ID number was 0-098451. This information is included here for future reference should anything ever be found.

Perhaps there is a hunter or hiker somewhere who knows of some twisted pieces of metal lying in the woods that they have never thought twice about. To the untrained eye, aviation crash sites are hard to recognize, especially when an airplane has augured into the ground at two hundred miles per hour. Or maybe a fisherman or scuba diver is aware of a form resembling an airplane at the bottom of a lake that they just assume everyone knows about because it has always been there. Reporting such a find could be the key to solving the mystery of what happened to Lieutenant Cassidy.

THE CASE OF THE MISSING "SUB-KILLER"

1944

On the night of January 31, 1944, while the world was embroiled in the midst of World War II, a four-engine U.S. Navy aircraft left Quonset Point Naval Air Station with a crew of ten men aboard for what was to be a routine anti-submarine patrol. The plane flew off into the night and was never heard from again.

In the dark days of the war, Nazi U-boats wreaked havoc on Allied shipping convoys as they made their way from the United States to overseas ports carrying men and supplies vital to the war effort. As a way to combat the submarines, land-based aircraft carrying bombs and depth charges would routinely patrol the sea a few miles off the coast hoping to locate enemy vessels.

This particular aircraft had been built for the army as a B-24 Liberator but was turned over to the navy to become part of a specialized group of "sub-killers." The B-24 was designed to replace the famous B-17 "Flying Fortress." Although it lacked the graceful lines of the Fortress and was often referred to as a "flying boxcar" due to its relatively square shape, its heavier bomb capacity more than made up for its homely looks.

The navy redesignated the Liberator as a PB4Y-1 and gave it a makeover by changing its olive drab paint scheme to dark gull gray over white (the camouflage colors routinely used for Atlantic-based aircraft) and added top-secret radar equipment for locating surfaced submarines, thereby changing the role of the aircraft from high-altitude bomber to that of a "hunter-killer."

It had been snowing with strong gusty winds the night the PB4Y-1 vanished, and when it failed to return, naval officials assumed the crew had "ditched" in the sea. A search was organized, but resources were divided between looking for the lost plane and searching for a fishing boat in distress. Searchers were further hindered when the weather turned worse the following day.

It was January, and with the water temperature in the thirties, a man in the ocean didn't stand a chance. The only possibility for survival rested in getting into an inflatable life raft before the aircraft sank, but even then, adrift in an open raft that time of year only meant a slower death from exposure.

The chance recovery of this World War II aircraft propeller by a fishing boat dragging its nets off Block Island proved to be the key to solving an old mystery. *Courtesy of Lawrence Webster.*

Despite the best rescue efforts available, no trace of the missing plane was found. Coastal areas were put on the alert to search the shoreline for debris or flotsam, but again, nothing was found.

The official naval inquiry into the disappearance was brief. "In view of the fact that no trace of this plane has been found," the official report begins, "all findings are a matter of hypothesis."

The pilot, Lieutenant Hubert C. McClellan, of Plymouth, Michigan, was no rookie. He had received his pilot's rating in August 1941, and had nearly 1,600 hours of flight time when he disappeared. Investigators theorized that despite his flight experience, McClellan may have suffered vertigo brought on by the darkness of the night and lack of visual reference points, possibly compounded by the failure of key cockpit instruments like the artificial horizon. Another possibility included engine failure, but this was all speculation.

Investigators also took into account the plane's specialized mission of hunter-killer. The aircraft had been modified with top-secret radar equipment designed for locating submarines on the surface at night. World War II–era submarines were required to surface every so often to recharge batteries, vent foul air and transmit and receive radio messages. Due to anti-submarine patrols, the safest time to surface was at night, preferably when there was no moon.

It was the job of this PB4Y-1 to seek and destroy these subs. If one was located, the aircraft had a powerful searchlight mounted under the right wing with which to turn darkness into daylight. The plane would then swoop in and release its bombs or depth charges before the sub had a chance to submerge.

Operation of the searchlight was done by the copilot, a fact also considered by investigators who wondered if the copilot had been unable to assist at a critical moment of equipment failure. This possibility led to the recommendation that in the future, the duty of searchlight operations should be assigned to someone other than the flight crew. The PB4Y-1 was a difficult plane to fly under normal conditions, let along during a low-level attack.

Apparently, investigators didn't consider the possibility that the plane could have been lost due to hostile action, for it is not stated in the report.

With nothing more to go on, and a war to win, the investigation was closed pending new information. Next of kin were notified that their loved ones were missing and presumed dead. The rest of the squadron was transferred overseas, and the incident faded from memory.

Just over two months later, on April 6, 1944, the *Nathaniel B. Palmer*, a fishing trawler out of Stonington, Connecticut, met with a mysterious accident. The *Palmer* with its crew of four had been dragging its nets along the ocean bottom about thirteen miles southeast of Block Island when the nets snared an unexploded bomb, which blew up just under the boat. Only one man survived to tell the tale, which offered the first hint of what might have happened to the missing aircraft.

A few days later, the *George A. Arthur* brought up another unexploded bomb found in the same vicinity. Boats were cautioned to stay clear, but the area was known to be a rich fishing ground, so some ignored the warning. Over time, more bombs were recovered by other boats.

However, recovery of the bombs didn't solve the mystery of the missing sub-killer. It only suggested that it might have dropped them on a target and they failed to explode. Although there had been no reported sightings of submarines the night of the disappearance, that didn't mean enemy subs hadn't been lurking about.

The war ended, and more time passed.

Enter Lawrence Webster, an aviation archaeologist and historian in Charlestown, Rhode Island. Webster was born shortly after World War II ended and became interested in airplanes and aviation history at an early age. One day while in his early teens, his parents told him about a World War II plane wreck in the woods near their house and suggested Larry try to find it. He did, and that discovery piqued his interest enough to search out more wrecks. One by one, over the years, Larry documented the locations and circumstances of literally thousands of civilian and military plane crashes throughout New England. Today, his database contains what is perhaps one of the most complete inventories of New England aviation accidents in the world.

Webster holds a BS degree in mechanical engineering and is a member of the Quonset Air Museum. Knowing that fishing trawlers plying their trade in Rhode Island waters sometimes bring up aircraft wreckage in their nets, Webster advertised that he and his organization would be interested in anything they found.

Then came a day in April 1992, when the fishing boat *Nancy & Gary* out of Point Judith, Rhode Island, snared a three-blade propeller in its nets while dragging about thirteen miles off Block Island. It was obvious that the pitted and discolored prop had been in the water a very long time. Webster was contacted about the discovery and had the propeller brought to his home, where he could examine it more carefully. After dismantling the propeller's hub, he discovered a series of numbers stamped into the metal. Despite decades in salt water, the numbers were still clearly legible due to grease packing applied during the manufacturing process.

Through his own detective work, Webster discovered that the propeller had been manufactured by Hamilton Standard in Connecticut and that this particular model was only used on two types of aircraft: the C-47, a transport plane, and the B-24 Liberator, aka the PB4Y-1. His files indicated that only one B-24 Liberator/PB4Y-1 had been lost in the area where the propeller was found, and that was the one that disappeared in 1944. His next move was to try and locate the wreckage.

Webster contacted Paul Matthias, owner of Polaris Consulting Inc. in Narragansett, and John Perry Fish and H. Arnold Carr, of American Underwater Search and Survey, Ltd., of Cataumet, Massachusetts. Both companies had underwater side-scan sonar equipment capable of locating objects lying on the bottom of the sea. Intrigued at the possibility of solving a mystery, the men agreed to find the lost bomber if they could.

Working as a team, they began the search by using the approximate longitude and latitude coordinates supplied by the *Nancy & Gary* as a starting point. Assisting in the exploration were two survey vessels, the *Menemsha* and the *Phantom*, piloted by two experienced captains and deep-sea divers, Eva Longobardi and Peter Sachs.

After searching several square miles of ocean floor, wreckage belonging to the long lost PB4Y-1 was finally located. The debris field was scattered over a wide area, most likely due to fishing trawlers dragging their nets over the years.

Divers who explored the wreckage confirmed the paint scheme was that of a navy aircraft, and artifacts brought to the surface were later confirmed as belonging to a PB4Y-1.

Webster then notified the U.S. Navy of the find but was told that nothing would be recovered for fear of disturbing any large pieces of the aircraft that may still contain human remains. Webster and others attempted to track down surviving relatives of the lost crew, but their success was limited. Some families received closure; others did not.

Thus, the case of the missing sub-killer was solved, but the incident has once again faded into history. The PB4Y-1 and its crew still lie at the bottom of the Atlantic and always will. It is their monument, for there are no white tombstones in a veterans' cemetery to mark their graves nor any Rhode Island memorials commemorating the sacrifice they made to their country. But thanks to a dedicated group of people who never knew these servicemen, they will at least be remembered here.

Lieutenant Hubert McClellan, Plymouth, Michigan
Lieutenant Harold Leroy Neff, Centralia, Missouri
Ensign Niles D. Kinney, Woodlake, Minnesota
AMM1C Arthur Joel Lien, Hixton, Wisconsin
AMM1C Nathaniel Hornstein, Bridgeport, Connecticut
ARM3C Wilton Hardin, Elizabethtown, North Carolina
ARM3C Willard J. Hinger, Newark, Ohio
AMM2C Peter Yezersky, Hermine, Pennsylvania
ARM3C William J. Kline, Philadelphia, Pennsylvania
AOM3C John H. Linnehan Jr., Albany, New York

A D-DAY MYSTERY AT THE "DUMPLINGS"

1944

On the morning of June 6, 1944, the greatest military invasion of all time was taking place on the shores of Normandy, France. For hours, the world held its collective breath as the fate of the war hung in the balance, for if the invasion failed, the Allies could very well lose the war.

Meanwhile, the war was still being fought on the homefront, too, and at 9:30 a.m. (Eastern Standard Time), a U.S. Navy PV-1 Ventura took off from Quonset Point for Massachusetts with seven men on board. Just five minutes into the flight, the Ventura crashed into Narragansett Bay off Jamestown in an area known as the "Dumplings," so called due to the underwater rock formations there. Rescue boats quickly set out from shore, but all on board were lost.

Newspaper accounts of the incident were understandably brief due to the invasion. One witness recalled to reporters that there were two explosions aboard the aircraft, one in the air and a second upon impact with the water. He related that after the first explosion, the plane flipped on its back and entered the water upside down. However, the official navy crash investigation report does not support this. According to the report (Number 44-14865), the cause of the crash is listed as 85 percent pilot error and 15 percent poor weather conditions, even though it is stated elsewhere in the report, "The cause of the accident is undetermined as all personnel aboard were killed. Eye witness accounts and recovered wreckage disclosed no clues as to the cause of the accident."

What caused a U.S. Navy PV-1 Ventura similar to the one pictured here to suddenly fall out of the sky over Jamestown while the invasion of Europe was taking place? *Courtesy of Library of Congress, photo #LC-USW33-032361-C.*

It was speculated by the navy that the plane might have suffered engine trouble and the pilot had come down through the low cloud ceiling to get visual bearings. When he did so, he realized the plane was too low and improperly attempted to regain altitude. However, this was only speculation.

The only civilian aboard was Dr. John Morris of California. Why he was on that flight was never explained, but it is assumed that he was working on a project for the government. He was not a medical doctor but a PhD who had been a college professor and a consultant for the Pasadena, California police department in the area of forensic technology. He is credited with inventing a method for lifting latent fingerprints from items that otherwise would not be possible using traditional methods.

The discrepancies between the eyewitness account and the official navy report were never explained. Did the plane explode, or was the sound that was heard only the engines backfiring due to mechanical trouble? Recovered wreckage reportedly showed no sign of fire or explosion. The incident has been forgotten with the passage of time, but the questions remain.

ONE SECRET REVEALED, ANOTHER KEPT

1944

On November 29, 1944, a flight of four P-47 Thunderbolts out of Hillsgrove Army Air Field in Warwick were on a routine training flight when they entered a small cloud near the Rhode Island/Connecticut state line. The planes were only in the mist for three to five seconds, but when they emerged out the other side it was discovered that one plane had simply vanished. Finding it only added to the mystery.

Airplanes usually go down for three main reasons: pilot error, mechanical failure and weather—not necessarily in that order. During wartime, combat damage can be another cause, but that didn't happen in this case. So, if none of these reasons could explain why a perfectly sound U.S. fighter plane could simply fall out of the sky, what explanation is left?

The missing P-47 came down next to a house on School Street in the border town of Putnam, Connecticut. Rescue crews arrived on scene and notified military officials. Although there was plenty of wreckage to be found, there was no pilot. The mystery deepened when some eyewitnesses on the ground reported that they believed they saw the pilot still in the plane just before impact. Nobody reported seeing a parachute. A backhoe was brought in to excavate the site, but despite digging down for fifteen feet, no trace of the pilot was located.

Officials were stumped. The weather that morning was seasonable for November in New England, with general cloud overcast. Conditions may not have been ideal, but they were hardly bad enough to cancel flying for that day.

When a perfectly sound army fighter plane simply vanished from formation on a training flight, it sparked an investigation, the results of which have been kept secret since World War II. Now the story can be told. *Illustration by Bill Gallagher Jr.*

Army investigators sift the wreckage looking for clues to the missing pilot. This photo is from the official army investigation report.

The four planes had taken off from Hillsgrove about 9:00 a.m. for what was to be a gunnery training flight. The only hint of trouble lay in the fact that the missing pilot had inexplicably delayed taking off for five minutes after the others had left the ground. The flight leader was an experienced captain who led the formation followed by the other three planes. The missing twenty-five-year-old pilot had held the fourth position in the flight.

The flight had proceeded to Point Judith, Rhode Island, but found weather conditions there unacceptable for target practice, so the planes turned north and headed for Massachusetts. As they neared Glocester, Rhode Island, they encountered a small cloud at their altitude and flew through it at two hundred miles per hour. When they emerged out the other side, they discovered the number four plane had disappeared.

Speculation as to what happened to the pilot focused on the probability that he had bailed out of the aircraft and that his parachute had failed to open, but this begged the question of why he would have left the aircraft in the first place.

The pilot's body was found two days later, half submerged in a swampy area about a quarter of a mile from the crash site, his parachute still strapped to his back, unopened. The discovery of the body was reported in one brief paragraph in a Putnam newspaper. This was the last the public ever heard of the incident, as more important wartime stories dominated the media. One detail omitted in the newspaper was the fact that the pilot had been found with his brain missing.

The rest of this story was gleaned from the now declassified army crash investigation report of the incident and is told here publicly for the first time.

Normally, it would have been assumed that the pilot was killed when he hit the ground; however, a medical officer determined that the injuries to the pilot's head were caused by the plane's rear stabilizer striking him as he exited the aircraft. The head injury would have been instantly fatal, which explained why the ripcord to the parachute had never been pulled. Yet officials noted that the pilot was no rookie and certainly knew the proper way to leave an aircraft. How, then, had he made such a simple mistake?

An investigation board was convened consisting of five army officers. They interviewed dozens of witnesses and examined aircraft maintenance records, as well as pieces of the wreckage, but found nothing to explain why the pilot had jumped from the plane. In their search for answers, the committee looked into the pilot's service record. By all accounts, he was an excellent pilot. He had flown numerous combat missions in the South Pacific and had only recently returned to the United States to become a flight instructor.

Delving deeper, it was discovered that the pilot had bailed out of an aircraft once before under similar circumstances while over New Guinea. This was found to be significant. In speaking with fellow officers who knew him personally, the board learned that the pilot had an abnormal fear of instrument flying, and it seemed that he had successfully avoided it during his training and flight career. Instrument flying is when a pilot has to rely solely on his cockpit instruments to maintain a safe course and altitude when all visual references have been obscured, such as when flying in thick cloud cover or fog. The pilot's service record showed that he had been checked out for instrument flying in April 1943, but the records did not indicate that he had ever actually logged any instrument flight time or obtained his instrument flight rating.

Perhaps his training had "slipped through the cracks" because the pilot had entered service at the beginning of World War II, when the army needed pilots in a hurry. By April 1943, he was already a combat veteran serving in a combat theater, and grounding him for failing to attain an instrument rating would have been counterproductive under the circumstances.

It was surmised by the accident investigation board that the cause of the accident was due to the pilot having an extreme phobia of flying into clouds where he would be forced to rely on instruments. It was also determined that had he stayed with his plane, he would have been out of the cloud in a few seconds and would most likely have remained close enough to keep the other aircraft in sight. The board did not overlook the fact that the pilot may have been suffering from the effects of combat, what we would today refer to as post-traumatic stress disorder.

Thus, it wasn't the weather, mechanical failure, pilot error or even hostile fire that brought the young aviator's plane down that cold November day. It was fear. Phobias come in many forms, and many people have them. Those who live with them will tell you that they are very real, at least to them, and they can be paralyzing.

The reader has no doubt taken note of the fact that the pilot's name and other identifying information have been omitted from this story. This was done intentionally out of respect for him and his family. It should also be noted that even though it was an extreme fear that led to his death, his combat record proves that he was no coward, and he died while in the service of his country.

RESCUE AT SEA

1948

The Atlantic Ocean is vast and deep, and searching for the crew of a lost aircraft can be like looking for the proverbial needle in a haystack: a tiny speck in a massive field of moving water that can actually become totally invisible to the tired eyes of a searcher who has stared at it for hours. The crew of a downed U.S. Naval aircraft was forced to consider this as they bobbed in the water one hundred miles off the coast of Rhode Island. To the cold and wet crew, the frigid, gray water seemed endless, but at least they were alive—for the time being.

The drama began about 6:25 p.m. on April 23, 1948, when a U.S. Navy P2V Neptune was on the last leg of a round-trip navigational flight from Quonset Naval Air Station to Bermuda and back. The plane was at twelve thousand feet and one hundred miles from home when the right engine suddenly developed a vibration problem. Cockpit gauges indicated low manifold and oil pressure. While the crew was trying to determine the cause, the left engine began experiencing the same difficulty. As oil pressure dropped in both engines, friction began to heat the metal pistons, and before long the vibration became severe. Shortly afterward, flames began licking out of the right engine cowling, but the onboard fire suppression system did little to cool the now red-hot metal. It became obvious that the plane wouldn't remain airborne much longer.

Even in late April, the Atlantic can be cold and forbidding, and ditching in the sea is never a pleasant thought for any aviator, for planes don't float for long. However, there was no choice, for at any moment the engines could seize, causing a propeller to rip loose and tear into the cabin or, worse, cause a wing to fold. The pilot, Lieutenant Harvey H. Rouzer, cut power to both engines, feathered the props to reduce drag and alerted his crew to stand by for an emergency water landing. Radioman William Delligatti sent an SOS to Quonset and switched the emergency locator on. The question was, would the signals be heard?

Gliding down from the sky, Rouzer saw an oil tanker steaming below and hoped it might see his stricken aircraft and come to its rescue. Unfortunately, the plane was gliding downward at one thousand feet per minute, and at that rate, the Neptune would be miles away when it hit the water. (It was later determined that nobody aboard the tanker had seen the aircraft go down.)

The Neptune continued downward. The now silent but red-hot engines glowed against the evening sky, trailing oily smoke as if it were a contrail. It took all the skill Rouzer could muster to keep the plane steady against cross winds as the mocking sea loomed closer and closer. Just before impact, the pilot skillfully raised the nose and turned into the wind to make the landing as soft as possible. Fortunately, the sea was relatively calm, with four- to five-foot swells that allowed for such a landing. Almost immediately, the crew began scrambling out; Rouzer and his copilot, Ensign Phillipe Fagan, crawled through escape hatches above their seats and the rest of the men through the astro-navigation hatch at the top of the fuselage. Standing on the wings as the water washed over them, the men struggled to free the two emergency life rafts from their outside compartments. One came out rather easily, and when the inflation cord was pulled, the CO_2 canisters inside rapidly inflated the raft. The other raft, however, seemed stuck, and as the pilot struggled with it the plane suddenly broke in two just behind the wings and rapidly began filling with water. As the tail tipped upward and the nose sank downward, the men had to jump clear before the suction of the sinking aircraft could pull them under. Within seconds, the five crewmen found themselves in the chilly water with only one life raft that was built to hold a maximum of four men.

For the moment, they were safe, but now the discussion turned to who would get into the raft and for how long, for the cold water would soon bring on hypothermia, and one's only chance rested with being able to get out of the water. While the logistics of the problem were being calculated, as if by a miracle, the plane's other inflatable raft suddenly bobbed to the surface, having somehow pulled itself free from its compartment when the plane hit the bottom. Once it was inflated, both rafts were tied together.

By now it was nearly dark. The men were cold and wet but otherwise uninjured. The greatest danger was hypothermia, and with night coming on the temperature began falling. Some, no doubt, wondered if they could survive the night, but none wanted to show fear to the others. They kidded each other. They made jokes. They even sang songs like "Anchors Aweigh" to keep their spirits up. There was nothing more they could do but hope their distress signal had been received. Unbeknownst to them, it had, and as they lay in the rafts bobbing in the sea, two rescue planes had already been dispatched from Quonset Point.

After about two hours, the men saw the lights of another ship looming on the horizon and lit a handheld signal flare, but the ship sailed on and gave no indication that the flare had been seen. Then a rocket flare was fired, but it, too, was ignored by the ship. One who has never been to sea might ask how this is possible, but there are several possibilities—however, none that would make anyone in that situation feel better.

The downed airmen fired a rocket flare signaling for help, yet remarkably, the ship sailed on. *Illustration by Bill Gallagher Jr.*

As the men watched the ship sail over the horizon, they could at least find comfort in the thought that they were in shipping lanes and another vessel could pass by at any time. Although the lookouts aboard the ship had failed to see it, the rocket flare had been seen by one of the rescue planes, which changed course to investigate. Lieutenant Rouzer described what happened next as being "just like in the movies," as the rescue plane zoomed directly over their heads and dropped six flares all about the rafts to light the way for other rescue craft.

As this was happening, a passenger liner, the SS *Washington*, came into view. The captain saw the flares being dropped in the sea and assumed it was a drill being conducted by the navy. It wasn't until one of the rescue planes flew circles around his ship that he realized the situation was real. He changed course for the flares and arrived at the scene at 10:20 p.m., just about four hours after the crew splashed down in the water. Once the rescue was complete, the *Washington* continued on to its destination in New York, where it arrived the following morning.

This wasn't the first time the *Washington* had experienced an adventure on the high seas. On June 11, 1940, several months before the United States entered World War II, the *Washington* was stopped by a German U-boat off

A P2V Neptune undergoing restoration at Rhode Island's Quonset Air Museum. The Neptune was a big airplane: 91 feet long, with a 103-foot wingspan. *Photo by author.*

the coast of Portugal. The captain was told he had ten minutes to abandon ship and get his 1,600 passengers and crew into lifeboats before the ship was torpedoed. To get everyone off the ship in such a short span of time was impossible, yet there was no choice. As preparations were being made, the U-boat commander abruptly departed without any explanation and let the ship sail on.

A few months later, the *Washington* was appropriated by the U.S. government and converted to a troop carrier. Throughout the war, it was under constant threat of torpedoes as it made repeated convoy runs between the United States and England. It returned to service as an ocean liner in 1946, which is how it happened to be on hand to rescue the downed airmen.

The P2V Neptune was developed at the end of World War II as an anti-submarine patrol aircraft to replace earlier aircraft used by the navy. The Neptune entered service too late to be widely used in World War II, but it was used extensively by the navy up through the Vietnam War.

According to the Quonset Air Museum, of the 1,181 Neptunes produced, only about 40 are still in existence, making it a rare war bird today. At the time of this writing, the Quonset Air Museum is in the process of restoring a Neptune.

THE STRANGE DISAPPEARANCE OF LIEUTENANT COMMANDER ALBERT FOSTER

1949

In the spring of 1949, military and civilian authorities including the Rhode Island Civil Air Patrol took part in the largest tri-state search and rescue operation ever conducted in southern New England. The search was for a missing navy airplane that had suddenly and mysteriously disappeared over Rhode Island. To this day, the mystery remains only half solved.

The incident began on the foggy night of March 23, 1949, with a distressed radio message transmitted by Lieutenant Commander Albert D. Foster of Weymouth, Massachusetts, who reported he was in trouble somewhere over the Providence metropolitan area. "I'm going over the side—I'm running low on gas," he reported. The garbled message was received at 7:20 p.m. by a radio control operator at Squantum Naval Air Station, who immediately notified his superiors. These were the last words ever heard from Foster.

Quonset Point naval authorities instituted an immediate search and rescue operation, but they were stymied by the fact that nobody had reported any downed aircraft.

Lieutenant Commander Foster was an experienced pilot. He was a combat veteran of World War II who had earned six Air Medals and the Distinguished Flying Cross twice. During the war, he served aboard the aircraft carrier USS *Lunga Point* in command of a fighter squadron. Therefore, it can be assumed that he was a man of good judgment who was accustomed to dealing with stressful situations and was not one to panic.

On the night of his disappearance, Foster was part of a two-aircraft ferry mission flying F4U Corsairs from Quantico, Virginia, to Squantum Naval Air Station north of Boston. The Corsair was a reliable single-seat fighter used extensively by marine and navy pilots throughout World War II and even into the Korean War. Its fuel capacity should have been more than adequate to complete the flight, yet apparently it wasn't. Had a fuel line ruptured? There was no way to tell until the missing aircraft was recovered.

The second Corsair, piloted by Lieutenant Commander S. Larch Miller, eventually landed at Westover Air Force Base in Chicopee, Massachusetts. Miller reported that while they were flying over the Providence area, they had encountered what he described as "ragged conditions" and had circled the area trying to obtain a visual fix on their position. It is presumed that this may have burned up much of Foster's fuel supply. At some point the two planes became separated, and Miller found his way to Westover.

Authorities had hoped that Foster had also set down someplace safe, but when no word came, a massive air and ground search was launched. Military installations throughout New England were put on alert, and by the following morning over sixty aircraft and several Coast Guard vessels were taking part in the search. Military officials on the ground were assisted by local police and firefighters, as well as civilian volunteers.

As the news spread, concerned citizens began reporting that they had heard a plane in trouble the night before. Two Rhode Islanders reported to the Chepachet state police barracks that they had heard a plane with its engine sputtering heading toward the Buck Hill Management Area. A citizen in Massachusetts reported hearing the same thing followed by what he thought was a crash. These reports, and others, required the search to be expanded into Connecticut and Massachusetts. However, despite the massive effort, by the end of the day nothing had been found. It seemed that Foster and his plane had simply vanished.

On March 26, the search focused on a wooded area in Northbridge, Massachusetts, after two local men reported hearing faint cries for help coming from a boggy swamp above the Rice City Dam. They said they had been hunting when their dog suddenly ran off toward the swamp and began barking at the water's edge while looking toward the wooded area beyond. As they came up behind the dog, they could hear faint cries for help coming from the distance. They called back, received answers and tried to pinpoint where they were coming from, but the cries grew fainter and weaker and finally stopped altogether. Based on this new information, a massive ground

Two hunters reported hearing faint cries for help coming from a swamp, yet searchers found nothing. *Illustration by Bill Gallagher Jr.*

search involving hundreds of personnel crisscrossed the area, but again no trace of Foster was found.

In the meantime, pieces of aircraft wreckage were snared in the nets of a fishing boat that had been dragging its nets off the coast of Gloucester, Massachusetts, in an area where the water is over two hundred feet deep. Apparently the wreckage hadn't been in the water for very long, for there was no sea growth on it, and serial numbers on the aircraft positively identified it as Foster's. However, the discovery raised more questions than it answered.

The metal was so twisted and bent that naval authorities concluded that the plane had crashed into the sea and hadn't "ditched" in an emergency landing. This led them to believe that Foster might have parachuted from the plane beforehand, yet there was still no trace of him. Had he drowned and his body been carried out to sea? How could the plane be north of Boston when Foster reported he was bailing out over Rhode Island?

Investigators theorized that Foster may have bailed out over northern Rhode Island or southern Massachusetts and his plane continued on without a pilot before crashing. One might ask how that was possible considering the Corsair didn't have an autopilot and was reportedly so low on fuel that its pilot had to bail out. Yet what other explanation is there?

Then there were those cries for help in the woods of Northbridge. Were they a hoax or someone's sick idea of a joke? The two hunters were well known in the community as reliable and sober men and were not prone to exaggeration. It is likely that they definitely heard something, but was it actually Foster they heard calling for help?

The search was officially called off on March 27 after a volunteer search plane ran out of fuel and crashed in Norfolk, Massachusetts, although there were some public-spirited citizens who continued to search on their own. To this day, nothing more has ever been found.

What became of Lieutenant Commander Foster has never been positively determined. Navy officials commented that if his parachute had failed to open, it was possible Foster came down in a body of water, such as a swamp, and sank into the muck at the bottom. If his chute did open, he might have been seriously injured on landing and eventually succumbed to exposure. In either case, Lieutenant Commander Foster is still officially listed as "missing—presumed dead."

"THIS IS NOT A DRILL!"

1954

May 26, 1954, was a solemn homecoming for the USS *Bennington* as it sailed into Quonset Point. Wisps of white smoke could be seen coming from below decks as tugboats maneuvered it into position for mooring. There were no bands playing; no cheering crowds of welcoming family and friends. Instead, rows of ambulances lined the dock waiting to take away the wounded. The deck rails of the carrier were lined with grim-faced crewmen clad in dirty work clothes instead of traditional dress whites, their faces blackened from soot and glistening from sweat. Typically when a ship of war returns from the sea it is a festive occasion, a cause for celebration, but this homecoming was part of a living nightmare. More than one hundred of the crew were dead or dying, and over two hundred others had been injured, and our country was not at war.

A few hours earlier, the *Bennington* had been steaming just south of Newport, Rhode Island, on a routine training cruise conducting normal ship operations. A United States aircraft carrier is a virtual floating city, and like most cities, it never sleeps. Shortly before 6:00 a.m., flight operations were begun as a line of fighter jets waited along the flight deck for their turn to launch. One by one, launch catapults hurled the jets down the length of the deck and into the morning sky. The first squadron was airborne by 6:10 a.m.

The catapults could be noisy for those with sleeping quarters situated nearby. While some had no problem with sleep during launch operations,

The USS *Bennington*, pictured here, suffered one of the worst peacetime disasters in U.S. Naval history. *U.S. Navy photo from the collections of the Naval Historical Center #NH 97582.*

others found it impossible. Such was the case for Commander Clyde Norman, one of two ship's doctors, who decided to get dressed and leave his quarters even though he wasn't scheduled to be on duty. Just as he was making his way to the chow line, the ship was rocked by an explosion.

Ensign Robert Grant of Brooklyn, New York, was below decks in the forward hangar bay when the blast occurred, followed almost immediately by the alarm for "general quarters." As the crew raced to their assigned stations, it quickly became apparent that this was not a drill.

Ensign Grant later recalled seeing five crewmen run toward a forward hatch and begin pulling on it, but the door wouldn't open, so they put their might into it. Just then, a second explosion tore through the ship and blew the door inward; the blinding flash enveloped and vaporized the men. Grant later told reporters, "The five guys just vanished."

The forward hangar deck quickly filled with thick smoke, which cut visibility and made it hard to breathe. Grant and the others formed a human chain to keep everyone together as they made their way topside to the flight deck.

Commander Norman's decision to rise early had been a good one, for it saved his life. When general quarters sounded, he raced to his post in sick bay at the rear of the ship and prepared for the casualties that he knew would be coming. What he didn't know was that the only other ship's doctor was already dead, and he would have to rely on hospital corpsmen to help save patients. Before long, sick bay was overwhelmed with the injured, forcing Norman to move his base of operations to the aft hangar deck.

Meanwhile, others rushed forward to battle the flames or assist with rescue operations. One of those was Aviation Machinist Mate Francis Toth, of Phoenixville, Pennsylvania, who stated later, "I just couldn't stand there. I had to help." Dead bodies and debris littered the smoke-filled passageways as crewmen fought their way forward into the flames to save their shipmates.

Quartermaster James F. Witham of Somerville, Massachusetts, found the escape hatch from his compartment blocked by the injured and dead lying on the other side. He later related, "We couldn't open the escape hatch to help them and the heat was terrible."

Some of the crewmen who weren't killed outright found themselves cut off and trapped. Seaman Edward Cushman of Milford, Connecticut, related how he and two others tried to give encouragement via telephone to several shipmates trapped in a forward compartment. The trapped sailors pleaded for rescue before their air ran out, but the fire was too intense for firefighters to reach them quickly. The men were advised to lie on the floor and put wet rags over their faces, but this did little good. Cushman remained on the phone with one man until the end. In his final words, the unidentified sailor told Cushman, "This is my last breath." By the time firefighters reached the compartment, all had suffocated. Other bodies were found in the forward mess and the warrant officers' wardroom.

It wasn't just heat and flames that rescue men had to contend with; bombs and rockets had been jarred loose from their positions and had to be tossed overboard before they could explode.

Bennington's skipper, Captain William F. Raborn Jr., took charge of the situation by setting course for Quonset point and ordering the rest of the ship's aircraft into the air to clear the flight deck for rescue operations. Soon after the flight deck was cleared, land-based helicopters began arriving to evacuate the critically wounded. By 11:00 a.m., the ship was arriving in port. Even as it docked, fire crews were still at work below decks.

By 3:45 p.m., the first casualty reports were released: 79 dead, 220 injured. The list of dead would eventually grow to 103, making the *Bennington* disaster one of the worst peacetime accidents to occur in the history of the United States Navy.

One of those assigned to investigate the disaster was Admiral Robert Carney, chief of naval operations. He described the blast damage as "freakish and unique," adding that he had never seen anything like it before. Some places, he said, showed the effects of "tremendous pressure," while others showed signs of "complete vacuums." Some items showed the effects of heat, while similar items in proximity did not.

Investigators determined that the cause of the disaster was a leak in the pressurized hydraulic fluid system of the ship's aircraft launch catapults. The flammable hydraulic liquid had vaporized and the fumes had ignited, causing an explosion. The *Bennington* disaster led the navy to abandon the use of hydraulic catapults in favor of steam catapults like the ones in use by the British navy. A *Time* magazine article dated July 12, 1954, stated that the primary reason for the change was not just for safety but also because the steam catapults were faster and more powerful.

The *Bennington* was a World War II–era ship that saw action in the Pacific Theater. After the war, it was put in "mothballs" but was reclassified and recommissioned during the Korean War in 1952. Though the ship had lost its share of crewmen due to enemy action during World War II, it had also lost men due to accidents since its recommissioning. In April 1953, one of the ship's boilers exploded, killing eleven and injuring four. Not long afterward, a plane crashed into the forward flight deck, killing one and igniting a fire. In another accident, two men were killed when a jet crashed into a gun emplacement.

A year after the calamitous explosion, the secretary of the navy recognized 178 *Bennington* crewmen for their actions during the disaster. The *Bennington* carried a crew of 2,800 men. Therefore, it is probable that many more stories of courage and heroism from that day have yet to be told. Those who were there will deny they are heroes and say that they were simply men doing their duty. At the award ceremony, Captain Reborn had the utmost praise for every member of his crew.

Repairs on the *Bennington* were completed by the summer of 1955, and after a two-month shakedown cruise, it was classified fit for duty and sent to the Pacific. It continued faithful service into the Vietnam War, but by the end of the 1960s, it was considered obsolete and was decommissioned for the second time in January 1970. It was once again mothballed until such time as it might be needed.

The 872-foot-long *Bennington* had been built at a time when the entire world was at war, and for its day it was state-of-the-art. However, despite the many upgrades it had received over the years, computer technology developed during the 1980s, combined with newer aircraft that required longer flight decks, made it clear to the navy that it was hopelessly obsolete. It was therefore stricken from naval rosters in 1989 and scrapped in 1994.

TEN DAYS BEFORE CHRISTMAS

1958

It was ten days before Christmas 1958, and it was snowing over southern New England. As snow collected on tree branches, creating a winter wonderland, some turned their thoughts to a white Christmas. Fluffy snow has a way of muffling sound, making the world seem quiet and peaceful. Perhaps that's why when the sound came it was so startling. Some described it as dry branches snapping or a big tree falling. Others said they heard a loud roar followed by a sharp bang. Everyone who heard it knew that something bad had happened—a large airplane had gone down.

The aircraft was a twin-engine Lockheed Learstar, owned by the Johnson & Johnson Pharmaceutical Company of Brunswick, New Jersey. The plane was only three years old, an updated version of the Lockheed Lodestar, considered a luxury plane for the day. All seven people aboard the plane lost their lives, making this accident perhaps the worst civilian aviation disaster in terms of loss of life to ever occur on Rhode Island soil. (What is believed to be the worst civil aviation accident to occur in Rhode Island *waters* involved a commuter flight with the loss of eight lives in 1989.)

On the morning of December 15, the flight left Linden, New Jersey, bound for Logan Airport in Boston with five passengers and a crew of two. The passengers were all top Johnson & Johnson executives heading to a meeting at its LePage Glue Division.

Snow had been predicted, but for later in the day, so it came as a surprise when the plane encountered a snowstorm over Massachusetts.

This 1958 North Smithfield plane crash took the lives of seven people, thereby making it one of the state's worst civil aviation accidents to date. *Courtesy of the* Woonsocket Call.

When the plane reached Logan, officials informed the crew that the airport was closed due to icy conditions and diverted the flight to Beverly Municipal Airport just north of Boston. When the aircraft reached Beverly, the air traffic controller reported that the airport was also closed due to weather. At that point the pilot, Alexander Sable, turned the plane back toward New Jersey.

As the plane made its way southward, it began experiencing engine trouble. While passing over the town of Franklin, Massachusetts, Sable radioed a distress call saying that one engine had lost all power. This was the last word ever heard from the aircraft.

A broken wristwatch on one of the victims set the exact time of the crash at 9:45 a.m. *Courtesy of the* Woonsocket Call.

Courtesy of the Woonsocket Call.

With only one engine still operating, the Learstar began losing altitude, and the crew probably began searching for a place to make an emergency landing. However, the low cloud ceiling of only four hundred feet, combined with swirling snow, would have prevented the crew from finding visual reference points on the ground. It was later speculated that the pilot may have been trying to find North Central State Airport in Smithfield, but this was never confirmed.

Flying in such whiteout conditions can lead to disorientation. Perhaps the plane was lower than the crew realized, or perhaps they hoped to spot a visual reference point by dropping below the clouds. In any case, the Learstar passed low over a gas station owned by John Roberts at Primrose Four Corners. (Today it is a funeral home.) Roberts was inside doing paperwork when he heard the plane's engines sputtering and then a loud boom. The time was 9:45 a.m. The plane had gone nose first into a swampy, wooded area between Farnum and Douglas Pikes, about three and a half miles short of the runway at North Central Airport.

North Smithfield's chief of police, Joseph Freitas, received word of the accident via several phone calls and went to investigate. There had been no explosion or fire to help indicate where the wreckage was located, and it

Courtesy of the Woonsocket Call.

wasn't until later, when he saw a National Guard plane circling overhead, that he knew where to look.

The chief was among the first to arrive at the crash site, where he found one man still barely alive, lying with his lower extremities in a pool of icy water mixed with aviation fuel. Freitas carefully pulled him free and laid him on dry land, but he died a short time later. Crews from the North Smithfield Highway Department used heavy equipment to clear a roadway to the site, which was about a half mile into the woods.

Reverend Thomas Myrick, pastor of Saint John's Church in Slatersville, arrived to administer last rites. The dead were listed as Alexander Sable, the pilot; Edward Luidcinaitis, the copilot; and passengers Nelson A. Bergstend, Ferdinand Liot, Stephen Baksal, Raymond Buese and Jesse Hackney, all from New Jersey.

Investigators determined that the cause of the crash was due to ice forming in the carburetors of the engines.

This accident served as a lesson for all big business corporations not to transport all top executives on the same aircraft. It is for this reason that many corporations today fly their executives on separate flights.

There are few today who are even aware that this terrible tragedy took place, as the incident has all but been erased from local memory. The site itself has also been wiped away, and a sand and gravel company now occupies the land where the Learstar went down.

WHEN A SCORPION STRIKES

1959

There is much in life that we take for granted, always supposing that we are in control of our own destinies and that one day will always be like the next unless we wish it to change. For example, when we go to work, we always envision that we will come home. Then something unexpected happens that alters everything.

The morning of May 19, 1959, dawned like any other over Otis Air Force Base in Falmouth, Massachusetts. Lieutenant Robert J. Scearce Jr. of Portland, Oregon, had been on duty all night and was understandably waiting for his relief-man to arrive so he could go home. He checked his watch and looked toward the brightening sky, thinking about what he would do with his time off.

He was an aircraft radar observer attached to the Fifty-eighth Fighter Interceptor Squadron of the Strategic Air Command. Their job was to fly fighter jets, specifically F-89 Scorpions, to protect our nation from potential attack. It was necessary but sometimes boring duty. He was happy to see his relief arrive on time, but when the relief-man asked for a favor—to cover for him for an hour while he went to register his car—Scearce agreed. It was a decision that would alter the rest of his life.

The young lieutenant settled in as the day shift took over, hoping his friend's errand wouldn't take too long. A half hour later, the "scramble horn" went off, indicating an unidentified aircraft had entered New England

The F-89 Scorpion, like the one pictured here, got its name from its tail configuration, which some said looked like a scorpion about to strike. *Courtesy of National Museum of the U.S. Air Force, #060829-F-1234S-048.*

air space. Scearce and a pilot, Captain Arthur Cannella, ran to their waiting aircraft and immediately took off, followed by a second F-89.

In 2004, Lieutenant Scearce recalled that long-ago day: "Within minutes we were airborne and in contact with the GCI site which would vector us to the unidentified aircraft. Shortly after takeoff, we were in the clouds using IFR [instrument flight rules] and were being vectored by the GCI controller. After about fifteen minutes, I picked up the aircraft on my radar and gave Captain Cannella vector information to intercept the aircraft."

The F-89 Scorpion was considered state-of-the-art in the 1950s. It could fly 636 miles per hour, which wasn't considered particularly fast for that era. But what made the aircraft ideal for coastal defense was its advanced radar system, which could detect other aircraft up to 50 miles away.

Both Scorpions quickly found themselves flying in thick clouds that went all the way up to forty thousand feet, necessitating them to rely on instruments. Captain Cannella's F-89 was designated the radio call sign "Kilo November Nine" and the other F-89 was designated "Kilo November Ten." Even though both jets were scrambled out of Massachusetts, they were put in radio contact with the New York Air Defense Sector, which was using the call sign "Occasion."

Kilo November Nine was given the assignment to close in on the unidentified target, while the other F-89 was assigned surveillance duty roughly ten miles off the wing. Both aircraft climbed to thirty-six thousand feet but were still flying blind, or "popeye" in Air Force jargon. Cannella and Scearce closed in toward the target guided by their radar and finally got close enough to identify the UFO as a U.S. Air Force B-47 bomber.

"Within a few minutes, we could see the unidentified aircraft," Lieutenant Scearce related. "It was a B-47 Stratofortress obviously sent by SAC [Strategic Air Command] to test our defense capability. This occurred regularly to keep Air Defense Squadrons in first-rate readiness. It was the Air Defense Command's mission to protect all borders of the United States from any unidentified aircraft."

It was required that the intercepting aircraft read off the B-47's tail numbers as proof that they had located the right "bogey." After the tail numbers were transmitted, Captain Cannella was given permission to break off pursuit and return to base. Cannella acknowledged that he was breaking to starboard eighty degrees. This was the last transmission ever received from the crew of Kilo November Nine.

Lieutenant Scearce related what happened next:

> *Within seconds, I sensed that something was not right. The first thing I noticed was that the airspeed was increasing rapidly. Captain Cannella indicated he was having some trouble. The artificial horizon showed that our position was not what it should be, and the altimeter was spinning down rapidly. We finally broke out of the clouds, and the nose of the aircraft was pointed straight down. About this time, Captain Cannella informed me that the speed brakes were inoperative, and we should "Get the hell out." Later we found out the F-89 broke the sound barrier [760 miles per hour] as we streaked downward.*

Air Force policy was to eject in such a situation once the aircraft fell below ten thousand feet, the logic being that there was no way to recover from such a dive. When they fell below the cloud ceiling and saw the horizon line spanning across the top of the canopy, they knew it was time to bail out. The Plexiglas canopy disintegrated as explosive charges blew it into the nearly eight-hundred-mile-per-hour slipstream. For the crew, it was like slamming into a brick wall. Their helmets, boots, gloves and even wristwatches were torn from their bodies, and their flight suits were shredded. Each man also suffered dislocated shoulders and elbows, preventing them from controlling their parachutes, thus leaving them hanging helplessly in the air almost two miles up.

North Smithfield's chief of police, Joseph Freitas, stands next to one of the recovered ejection seats of the doomed F-89. *Courtesy of the* Woonsocket Call.

Lieutenant Scearce went on:

> *When I pulled the ejection handle, it felt like I had been kicked by a mule, and I momentarily blacked out. I saw that I was over a town, which turned out to be Woonsocket, Rhode Island. As I tried to reach for the risers of the chute, I realized that my arms didn't work* [he had two dislocated elbows] *so I was at nature's mercy. Not only was I injured, but the wind blast ripped off my watch and flight boots and shredded my flight suit.*

Meanwhile, those at Air Defense Command began to realize something was wrong when Cannella and Scearce suddenly disappeared from radar and attempts to contact them were unsuccessful. The following is taken from the radio transcript obtained from the now declassified Air Force crash investigation report:

> OCCASION: *"Kilo November Ten, your nine should now have gone off your starboard side. His last position that I had him was about fifteen your port side seven miles."*
>
> TEN: *"Roger, you still have no paint on him?"*

Occasion: "Negative, I'm not painting his parrot [not on radar], I lost him, you heard the last transmission that he made to us as he turned starboard."

Ten: "Roger, you want to clear me down through this stuff [the clouds], I'll drop on down here a little bit lower."

Occasion: "Ten that negative, be advised we're over land and if anything did happen to nine, no sense taking you down there too."

Kilo November Ten was given instructions to return to Otis Air Force Base.

Many on the ground witnessed the bailout, their eyes attracted skyward by the sonic boom created when the Scorpion broke the sound barrier, something it was not designed to do. Many assumed it was all part of the annual Woonsocket Mardi Gras celebration and returned to their daily routines.

Lieutenant Scearce landed hard on the roof of the U.S. Rubber Company on Fremont Street, breaking his hip and arm and suffering internal injuries. Remembering the landing, he said:

As I continued down, I saw that I was heading for a large building. I was later told that on the way down, I barely missed some high energy power lines. Shortly after, I hit the roof of the building, that turned out to be the four-story U.S. Rubber plant. I could not control the chute. It dragged me across the roof of the building before collapsing on the other side of a retaining wall. Ironically, the plant made mattresses.

Employees of the plant rushed to the roof via a fire escape and did what they could for the injured flyer until a fire department ambulance arrived and transported him to Woonsocket Hospital.

Meanwhile, Captain Cannella came down in Harris Pond next to the Precious Blood Cemetery. He became entangled in his chute lines and would have drowned had it not been for the quick actions of seventeen-year-old Roland Ruge, a cemetery employee, who swam out and pulled him to shore.

While the crew came down in Woonsocket, the doomed F-89 continued down into North Smithfield, crashing about a quarter of a mile from the Woonsocket line and exploding into a massive fireball. The concussion rattled windows and china of nearby homes, and flaming wreckage was scattered amidst a swath three hundred feet wide and nearly a half mile long.

Lieutenant Scearce being placed in an ambulance after being carried down from the roof of the factory. *Courtesy of the* Woonsocket Call.

A soldier stands guard over what remains of the F-89 cockpit. *Courtesy of the* Woonsocket Call.

Curious onlookers descended on the crash site, some of whom removed "souvenirs," which the Air Force demanded back. Some items were returned the following day, but others were not.

While both airmen were being treated at Woonsocket Hospital, Otis officials were given the task of notifying their wives. In 2004, Lieutenant Scearce's wife, Fran, recalled how she and Mrs. Cannella received the news:

The fire was so hot that some portions of the aircraft melted. *Courtesy of the* Woonsocket Call.

An investigator examines a portion of the charred tail section. *Courtesy of the* Woonsocket Call.

When the news came through that the crew had survived and was hospitalized in Woonsocket, Rhode Island, we were shaking and sighing at the same time. Originally Colonel Kress offered to fly Sarah and me to Woonsocket in a helicopter, but Mrs. Kress didn't think that was prudent because I was six months pregnant. So Sarah and I loaded her small Austin Healy Sprite and drove the hundred-plus miles. Sarah was calmer than I and a great support person in such a traumatic situation.

When we arrived that evening, we found the two men sharing the same hospital room. Bob looked grim. He had some scrapes and bruising on his face, and his arms and legs were virtually unusable. His elbows had been relocated, but the right one was obviously not properly put back in place, and he remains unable to straighten it to this day. His upper back thighs were pummeled by the life raft which was attached to his parachute. He was terribly bruised from that, and the windblast had flailed his legs, along with his arms unmercifully. Bob told me one morning that one of his legs had fallen out of bed and that he had to summon a nurse to put it back in bed!

The hospital staff was most accommodating and let Sarah and me stay in a room in a new wing which was not yet activated. I stayed several more days after the Cannellas returned to Otis AFB. The local Woonsocket residents were very hospitable. Several visited the men, brought small gifts and offered to lend a hand in any way.

One visitor to the hospital was Roland Ruge, who received sincere thanks from Captain Cannella for saving his life. The Air Force later gave Roland a special tour of Otis Air Base, a certificate of appreciation and a cockpit compass gauge from the wrecked F-89.

Captain Cannella later returned to full duty and spent many more years with the Air Force, eventually retiring with full honors. Unfortunately, Lieutenant Scearce discovered that his Air Force career was over. He had hoped to go to flight school and become a pilot; however, his injuries forced him to retire. He moved back to Oregon, where he became a science teacher and coach at Roosevelt High School in Portland.

Fran Scearce counts her blessings and summed it up best with the following: "There were many miracles about that May day in 1959. It is miraculous that both crew members survived, especially considering the airspeed into which they ejected. It is also unbelievable that the jet crashed into an uninhabited area so close to residences and a school and that there were no injuries on the ground."

GUARDIAN ANGELS

1962

Studies have shown that about two-thirds of the population believe in guardian angels, and the following story would seem to support the case for their existence. Was a benevolent force looking out for the Smith family (not their real name to protect their privacy) on the night of June 6, 1962, or was it all merely a lucky coincidence? You decide.

It was warm that evening, and four-year-old Susan Smith was playing outside the family home on Bound Road. (The road is so named because it sits directly on the boundary line of Woonsocket and Cumberland.) Being a typical four-year-old with ceaseless energy, Susan darted out into the street in front of an oncoming car. The driver no doubt had his heart in his throat as he stood on the brake pedal, hoping to avoid a tragedy. Fortunately, Susan was unhurt, but her parents were understandably upset.

Meanwhile, less than a mile away, Raymond LaPlante of Cumberland had just landed his small Luscombe airplane at Woonsocket Airport, which was located where Diamond Hill Plaza is today. He had just completed a test flight from North Central Airport in Smithfield after installing a new propeller. At Woonsocket, he met with nineteen-year-old Norman Lanctot, a fellow pilot and co-owner of the airplane, and the two discussed the recent modification.

Back at the Smith residence, the family was getting ready to settle in for the evening. Mr. Smith turned on the television in the living room and began getting Susan and her younger brother ready for bed while his wife attended

Some might call it "divine intervention," others "just pure luck." In either case, a seemingly insignificant event set in motion circumstances that led a family to leave their home just before an airplane crashed into it. *Courtesy of the* Woonsocket Call.

to other chores. For Mrs. Smith, the shock of Susan's near miss with the car hadn't worn off yet, so she announced that she had decided to go out to play beano (a game similar to bingo) because she needed to relax. A short time later, she left the house, leaving Mr. Smith in the living room with the children.

Susan herself was still fidgety and resisted her father's efforts to get her settled for bed, so on impulse, Mr. Smith took the children outside to the front yard to allow them to expel some energy. He would later tell a *Woonsocket Call* newspaper reporter that he didn't know why he had decided to do this.

As the children played on the front lawn, Smith saw two neighbors across the street working on a car in their driveway and waved hello. The time was now just before 8:00 p.m.

Back at the airport, LaPlante and Lanctot took off into the evening sky, but something went wrong as they became airborne, and the plane began losing speed and altitude. As it dropped from the sky, it headed directly toward Bound Road.

Smith's neighbors, still working on their car, saw the aircraft coming and shouted a warning. Smith had been standing with his back to them while watching his children and was unaware of the danger. He instinctively dropped to the ground just as the aircraft clipped a nearby tree, passed over his front yard and crashed into his living room. One of the children was hit by flying debris but, fortunately, suffered only minor injuries.

While Smith tended to his children, neighbors sprayed water from garden hoses onto the wreckage to prevent the highly flammable aviation fuel from igniting. When fire and police officials arrived and extricated the men from the plane, they found Lanctot dead and LaPlante seriously injured. The Luscombe was equipped with dual controls, and it was never positively established who was flying at the time of the accident.

Investigators examined the wreckage for clues. The plane had been completely overhauled and refurbished just three weeks earlier, with the new propeller added the same day as the accident. Fuel samples were sent out for testing, but no abnormalities were found. The cause of the crash was a mystery, but one thing is known for sure: Susan's chance encounter with a passing motorist most likely saved the lives of her entire family, for on any other night, the Smiths would have been sitting in their living room at the time of the crash.

The Smith home was eventually repaired, and today there are no apparent indications that such an accident occurred there. As for the Smiths, some might claim they were just lucky. Others might say that someone "up there" was watching out for them.

A FIRE ABOARD FLIGHT 458

1982

According to ancient Greek mythology, there once lived a man named Daedalus and his son Icarus, who were imprisoned by King Minos on the island of Crete. Being a man of innovation, Daedalus devised a method of escape by fashioning two sets of wings made of feathers and wax that they would use to fly like birds to Greece. Daedalus warned his boy not to fly too close to the sun lest the heat melt the wax of his wings, but once aloft, Icarus failed to heed the warning and fell to his death. Daedalus made it safely to Greece and erected a monument in memory of his son, and today, Icarus has come to symbolize all fallen aviators.

One of the more exciting tales in the annals of Rhode Island aviation concerns a fire that broke out aboard a Pilgrim Airlines commuter flight in 1982. Pilots are trained for such emergencies, but what happens when the fire erupts in the cockpit at four thousand feet? The crew of this plane was faced with two choices: die quickly in a horrible crash or burn to death in the hopes of saving the passengers. What would you have done?

The drama began on the afternoon of February 21, 1982, when Pilgrim Airlines Flight 458 took off from New York's La Guardia Airport headed for Boston with scheduled stops in Bridgeport, New Haven and Groton, Connecticut. At Groton, Captain Thomas N. Prinster, thirty-six, and First Officer Lyle W. Hogg, twenty-seven, relieved the crew that had flown the first leg of the journey. After leaving Groton at 3:10 p.m., the aircraft climbed to four thousand feet.

It took extraordinary strength and determination for the pilots of this flaming commuter aircraft to bring the plane down as fire burned their bodies and smoke choked their lungs. *Courtesy of the Potterville Fire Department.*

Fifteen minutes into the flight, Captain Prinster noticed ice forming on the windshield and activated the de-icer system, which utilized isopropyl alcohol as a de-icing agent. For some reason, the fluid didn't adequately spray the windshield, so he repeated the process and suddenly noticed a strong smell of alcohol beginning to permeate the cockpit, quickly followed by wisps of gray smoke coming from under the control panel. Realizing there was a fire on board, Prinster notified T.F. Green Airport that he needed clearance for an emergency landing.

Soon, toxic black smoke began billowing out from the control panel, filling the cockpit and making it hard for the crew to breathe. They slid the cockpit's vent windows open, but this had little effect, and as the smoke got thicker they found it impossible to read their instruments.

As the plane descended toward T.F. Green, smoke began curling back into the passenger compartment, causing alarm among the ten passengers seated there. One passenger came into the cockpit and, seeing flames licking out from under the control panel, tried to smother them with his coat, but the alcohol-fed flames could not be extinguished. He then grabbed another passenger's tennis racket and went to work smashing out the Plexiglas windows of the passenger cabin in an effort to vent the smoke. Other

113

passengers joined him and did what they could to assist, but all efforts were of little consequence.

Meanwhile, in the cockpit, the flames had ignited the clothing of the flight crew, beginning with their trouser cuffs and working their way upward. Despite the excruciating pain, the crew fought desperately to remain at their posts, for to abandon them meant certain death. As it was, their injuries might prove fatal, but at least the passengers stood a chance if they could find a place to set down before the flames consumed them, or they passed out from the smoke, or the plane lost all power and crashed.

In desperation, both pilots stuck their heads out the cockpit windows while still gripping the controls, but the cold February air, combined with a 160-mile-per-hour slipstream, presented other problems. While their faces froze, their legs burned.

Below them at 1,400 feet was a layer of overcast clouds that obscured all visual reference points on the earth below. Flying blind, and without their instruments to guide them, they were at risk of losing their sense of equilibrium. If that happened, they could crash straight into the ground, and everything would be over in an instant.

Despite the desperate situation, both pilots kept their composure and held the plane steady, knowing full well they would never make it to Green. Down they went toward the expanse of white cotton clouds, buffeted by cross winds, choking from smoke and burning from the fire. They had no idea what awaited them as they entered the scud—a hill, a building or open water. Breaking through at one thousand feet, they suddenly saw the wide expanse of the Scituate Reservoir before them, its water frozen and covered with snow. There was no way of telling if the ice could support the weight of an airplane, but there was no choice. The only alternative was a crash-landing in the heavy woods surrounding the reservoir—almost certain suicide.

Dropping to treetop level, the plane barreled in from the west as Prinster let down the landing gear. On touchdown, one of the plane's rear wheels punched a hole in the ice, ripping a portion of the landing gear away and sending the aircraft into a sideways skid. As the liner slid and bumped across the ice, a wing tore loose and slid away. The momentum carried the plane for more than five hundred feet before it finally came to rest in a secluded area of the reservoir.

The plane was still burning as passengers and crew scrambled out of the smoke-filled cabin onto the ice. Despite his pain and injuries, Captain Prinster remained in charge and showed leadership in keeping everyone together as

The aircraft was a De Havilland, Twin Otter, a small passenger liner designed to carry eighteen passengers and a flight crew of two. It was manufactured in 1967 and acquired by Pilgrim Airlines in 1972. *Courtesy of the Potterville Fire Department.*

A boat was brought onto the ice as a precaution. *Courtesy of the Potterville Fire Department.*

he led them toward shore. As they reached dry land, the first fire apparatus and police officers arrived on the scene. A quick headcount revealed that one passenger, Loretta Stanczak, fifty-nine, of New Hampshire, was missing.

Firemen made their way onto the ice toward the burning fuselage, but flames had all but consumed it by the time they could lay a hose line from the road out to the wreckage. The body of Mrs. Stanczak was later found still strapped in her seat.

The suspected cause of the accident was a defect with the aircraft's de-icing system pump that sent flammable isopropyl alcohol squirting onto electrical connections, sparking a fire. The system had been worked on as recently as three days before the accident.

Captain Prinster and First Officer Hogg were hailed as heroes for their actions. Prinster was admitted to Rhode Island Hospital in critical condition with burns over half his body, and for the next few weeks his life hung in the balance. Hogg, too, was badly burned, and both men required months of recuperation.

Captain Prinster was later awarded the Lieutenant General Harold L. George Civilian Airmanship Award by the Order of Daedalians for his efforts on that day. He and Lyle Hogg also received the Flight Safety Foundation Heroism Award. Both awards are very prestigious in the area of civil aviation.

A lasting memorial to this incident can be found at Prinster-Hogg Park, located at the intersections of Routes 102, 14 and Rockland Road, in Scituate, at a place referred to by locals as "Crazy Corners." It is near this site that Flight 458 came to rest. Hidden among the pines is a six-foot-high granite boulder inscribed with a summary of the event. The memorial is one of only four in the state dedicated to an aviation accident.

BIBLIOGRAPHY

Newspapers

Boston Herald. "1 Killed, 2 Pilots Missing Near Floyd Bennet Field," April 2, 1943, 18.
————. "Two Planes Crash in State," March 31, 1943, 7.
Cape Cod Standard Times. "Explosion of Otis Jet Being Probed," May 20, 1959.
————. "Investigation Is Continuing," May 21, 1959.
————. "Plane Crashes in Rhode Island," May 20, 1959.
————. "Plane Crash Kills Ten Men," December 9, 1943, 1.
Cape Cod Times. "Navy Plane Went Down in 1944 off R.I.," May 20, 1992.
Evening Bulletin. "Landing a Burning Plane with 12 Souls On Board," March 2, 1982, A1.
————. "Pilgrim Airlines Removes De-icers," March 2, 1982, A6.
————. "Quonset Death Toll Now Nine," December 6, 1943, 1.
————. "Seven Are Lost When Navy Plane Explodes in Air," June 6, 1944, 20.
————. "Two Lose Lives in Plane Crash at Smithfield," May 28, 1934.
Evening Reporter. "Conductor Opened Switch," October 10, 1895, 3.
————. "Funerals of the Victims," October 8, 1895.
————. "Inquest into Railway Wreck," October 10, 1895, 3.
————. "Into a Death Pit," October 7, 1895, 1.

Fall River Herald. "Navy Plane Crashes in Apple Orchard Here," March 31, 1943, 1.

Florida Times-Union. "Navy Aviator Dies in Crash," December 8, 1943, 13.

Lynn Telegram News. "Plane Falls into Sea off Swampscott Shore," March 31, 1943, 1.

Malden News. "F.P. Van Oosten Killed in Plane Crash," June 7, 1944.

Malden Press. "Malden Sailor Killed in Plane Crash," June 9, 1944, 5.

————. "Rescue Pair in Navy Plane Crash," March 31, 1943, 11.

Narragansett Times. "Loss of the *Metis*," September 6, 1872, 2.

————. "Scientists to View Plane Crash Site," May 29, 1992.

Naval Aviation News. "Ditching a Neptune," July 1948, 20.

New Platz Independent. "Three Wildcats Lost in Fog Make Emergency Landing on the Platz Flats Tuesday," April 1, 1943.

Newport Daily News. "Body of Army Pilot Recovered from Bay," February 12, 1943.

————. "Navy Plane Blows Up off Jamestown," June 6, 1944.

New York Times. "Bars Federal Men in Rum Ship Inquest," January 3, 1930.

————. "*Black Duck* Survivor Loses Boat to Guard," March 2, 1932.

————. "*Black Duck* Volley Wounds Rum-Runner," August 27, 1930.

————. "Cargo Craft Sunk," January 21, 1942.

————. "Coast Guard Guns Sink Rum-Runner," July 15, 1931.

————. "Coast Guards Held for Liquor Brawl," December 31, 1929.

————. "Coast Guard Shots Hit *Black Duck* Aft," January 4, 1930.

————. "Coast Guardsmen Wound Two in Seizing Boat off Woods Hole, but Find No Liquor Aboard," July 24, 1930.

————. "Concrete Ship Sinks in Collision off Newport; Goes Down in Three Minutes; 19 Missing," October 30, 1920.

————. "Concrete Vessel Crumbles in Wreck," October 31, 1920.

————. "Crowd Terrifies Coast Guard's Wife," January 7, 1930.

————. "Disaster on the Sound," August 31, 1872.

————. "Dry Men Get *Black Duck*," May 7, 1930.

————. "Enforcement Gone Wrong," January 8, 1930.

————. "15 Hurt in Wreck on New Haven Train," October 26, 1913.

————. "Five Dead in Wreck; Inquiries Begun," April 19, 1916.

————. "Flaw Ran through Rail," October 28, 1913.

————. "Gang of Men Beats 2 Coast Guardsmen," January 5, 1930.

————. "Jury on Rum Killing Absolves Coast Guard," January 15, 1930.

————. "Long Island," September 20, 1872.

————. "The *Metis*," September 2, 1872.

———. "The *Metis* Disaster," September 1, 1872.

———. "The *Metis* Disaster," September 4, 1872.

———. "The *Metis* Disaster," September 5, 1872.

———. "The *Metis* Disaster," September 8, 1872.

———. "The *Metis* Disaster," September 10, 1872.

———. "The *Metis* Investigation," September 13, 1872.

———. "More Liquor Found on Patrol Boats," January 6, 1930.

———. "Protests 'Orders' to Kill," January 4, 1930.

———. "Rear-End Crash on the New Haven Kills 8, Hurts 30," April 18, 1916.

———. "Rum Row Killings Upheld by Mellon," January 4, 1930.

———. "A Sad Story," September 3, 1872.

———. "Shots Stop Rum-Runner," February 26, 1930.

———. "Stop or Get Hurt, Billard Warns," December 30, 1930.

———. "A Supposed Victim of the *Metis* Disaster," September 7, 1872.

———. "Threatens Inquiry on Liquor Killings," January 1, 1930.

———. "Three on Rum Boat Slain by Coast Guard in Chase; Three Vessels Captured," December 30, 1929.

———. "Two Bodies Picked Up and Carried to Newport, R.I., with *Metis* Life-Preservers On," August 31, 1872.

———. "Upholds Coast Guard in *Black Duck* Killing," January 17, 1930.

———. "Wreck of the *Metis*," September 14, 1872.

———. "Wrecks Due to Neglect," June 16, 1916.

Pawtucket Times. "Plane Crashes Kill 2 Fliers, 3 Navy Craft Forced Down in Scattered Accidents," March 31, 1943, 5.

———. "Quonset Plane Crashes, 7 Die," September 5, 1951.

———. "Two Army Planes Collide over R.I.," October 31, 1942, 8.

Pawtuxet Valley Times. "Droves of Curious Trudge Miles to View Burnt, Broken Plane on Ice," February 22, 1982, 1.

———. "50 Planes Search for Missing Flyer," March 25, 1949, 1.

———. "Navy Experts Examine Plane Wreckage Found," March 26, 1949.

———. "Navy and Police Puzzled at Plane's Disappearance," March 24, 1949, 1.

Perham Enterprise Bulletin. "Luvern Klinger Fatally Hurt in Airplane Crash," December 9, 1943.

Providence Evening Bulletin. "48-year Mystery Solved?" May 19, 1992.

———. "Landing a Plane with 12 Souls on Board," March 2, 1982, A-1.

———. "Pilgrim Airlines Removes De-icers," March 2, 1982, A-6.

Providence Journal. "Army Digs in Vain to Find Pilot Who Dived into Brook in Putnam," November 30, 1944, 1.

———. "Eight Men Killed in Bomber Crash at Quonset," December 6, 1943, 1.

———. "4 Lost, 2 Rescued in Plane Mishaps," February 14, 1943, 5.

———. "Identification of Pilot Sought," July 12, 1958, 2.

———. "1 Dies, 11 Survive in Crash Landing," February 22, 1982, 1. West Bay Edition.

———. "Pilot's Message to Tower Reveals Nothing about Fire that Forced Crash Landing," February 22, 1982.

———. "Quonset Bomber Crashes in Ocean," April 24, 1948, 1.

———. "Quonset Fliers Describe Dramatic Rescue from Sea," April 25, 1948, 14.

———. "7 Thought Dead as Plane Crashes," June 7, 1944, 20.

———. "Tail of Felled Plane Is Retrieved; Investigators to Talk to Copilot," February 22, 1982, A3.

———. "Two Airmen Hurt Parachuting," May 20, 1959, 1.

———. "Two Army Pilots Lose Lives in Crashes in R.I., Two Other Planes in Unit Believed Lost," February 12, 1943, 1.

Putnam Patriot. "Tri-State Search for Missing Army Pilot," November 30, 1944, 1.

Quincy Patriot Ledger. "Leak in Dragger Forces Postponement of Plane Salvage," March 30, 1949.

——— "Navy Launches Search for Missing Weymouth Pilot," March 24, 1949, 1.

———. "Navy Planes Scan Coastline for Trace of Missing Flier," March 28, 1949, 1.

———. "Plane Wreckage Found at Sea," March 26, 1949, 1.

———. "60 Planes Continue Search for Missing Weymouth Flier," March 25, 1949, 1.

Stonington Mirror. "The Loss of the *Metis*," September 5, 1872.

St. Petersburg Times. "Hero Flier's Plane Found," March 27, 1949.

Time. "Armed Forces: A Better Slingshot," July 12, 1954.

———. "Education: Incident in Sydney," May 20, 1957.

———. "National Affairs: *Black Duck* Aftermath," January 13, 1930.

Westerly Sun. "Liberator Wreckage Found," May 27, 1992, 5.

Woonsocket Call. "AF, Pilot's Wife Pour Thanks on Hero Ruge," May 21, 1959.

———. "Air Crash Story Wrapped Up by Call While Presses Roll," December 16, 1958.

———. "Air Officer on Bennington Testifies in Blast Probe," June 1, 1953, 3.

———. "Another Body Recovered from Sunken Submarine, Increasing Rough Sea Halts Divers," October 3, 1925, 1.

———. "Bad Sea and Weather Conditions Force Temporary Suspension of Rescue Operations at S-51 Wreck," September 26, 1925, 1.

———. "Barking Arouses Attention," March 26, 1949.

———. "Bennington Docks at Quonset Point after Sea Tragedy," May 26, 1954. City Edition.

———. "Bennington Toll Climbs to 101—Probe Resumes," June 2, 1954.

———. "Block Signal Test Made by Officials at Bradford Wreck," April 22, 1916, 1.

———. "Bradford Signals Correctly Placed Declare Witness," April 21, 1916, 11.

———. "Bradford Wreck Hearing Started," April 20, 1916, 7.

———. "Carburetor Icing Seen Crash Cause," December 16, 1958.

———. "Carrier Disaster Death Toll 97 as Critically Burned Succumb," May 28, 1954, 1.

———. "Carrier Horror Probe Starts, Five from NE in 91 Death List," May 27, 1954. Worcester County Edition.

———. "Carrier Tragedy Recalls Recent Leyte Disaster," May 26, 1954, 1.

———. "Catapult Flaw, Navy Bugaboo, Looms in Bennington Disaster," May 27, 1954, 1.

———. "Concrete Vessel in Collision with Savannah Liner City of Atlanta; Three of 17 Rescued Injured," October 30, 1920, 1.

———. "Crash Pilot Blames 'Going too Fast,'" May 20, 1959.

———. "Crippled Plane Sought in Area," December 15, 1958, 1.

———. "Declares Kick May Unlock Switch," October 10, 1916, 2.

———. "Defective Boiler Blamed for Fatal Locomotive Blast," July 8, 1926, 18.

———. "Defective Signal May Have Caused Bradford Wreck," April 19, 1916.

———. "Destruction of Engine Throws 60-Car Freight in Path of Passenger Train," June 26, 1926.

———. "8 Die in Bomber Crash," November 21, 1952 .

———. "Eight Men Killed in Navy Plane Crash," December 6, 1943, 24.

———. "Engineer Mansfield Found Not Guilty," October 21, 1916, 1.

———. "Engine Failure Seen," December 15, 1858, 1.

———. "Expert Proposes Catapult Change," June 8, 1954, 1.

———. "Fatal Plane Crash Cause Still Sought," June 8, 1962.

———. "Five Persons Killed in Crash of New Haven Trains at Bradford; Over Thirty Others Are Injured," April 18, 1916, 1.

———. "41 Persons Seriously Scalded by Steam in Newport and Pawtucket Hospitals," August 19, 1925, 1.

———. "Giant Craneships Start Work of Raising Submarine S-51, Sunk off Block Island," October 1, 1925, 1.

———. "Grand Jury Will Start Probe into Bradford Wreck," April 21, 1916, 3.

———. "Grant Now Refuses to Testify Regarding *Mackinac* Disaster," September 3, 1925, 1.

———. "Guard of Honor on Duty at Bier—Wilkins Rites Tomorrow," May 29, 1934.

———. "Hospital Dietician Suddenly Stricken," May 31, 1934.

———. "Icing Probable Cause of Crash Which Killed 7," February 20, 1961, 27.

———. "Impressive Rites Held for Victims of Plane Crash," May 31, 1934.

———. "Investigators Seek Crash Solution," December 16, 1958.

———. "*Mackinac* Case Defendants Plead NOLO Imposing Sentence to Come Later," May 25, 1926, 1.

———. "*Mackinac*'s Sailing Delayed 45 Minutes," August 19, 1925, 1.

———. "Mystery Shrouds Plane Crash, Fire," October 31, 1942, 1.

———. "Navy Calls Off Uxbridge Area Hunt for Pilot," March 27, 1949.

———. "Navy Department Itself to Salvage Sunken Submarine," October 12, 1925, 1.

———. "Navy Starts Bennington Probe," May 29, 1954, 1.

———. "New Haven Railroad Issues Official Statement on Double Train Wreck," June 26, 1926.

———. "New Haven Road Has Third Wreck Within One Week," June 30, 1926, 4.

———. "Newport Man One of Missing Crew of Submarine S-51," September 25, 1925, 1.

———. "New Trial Ordered in *Mackinac* Disaster Case at Providence by Attorney General Sisson," June 2, 1926, 1.

———. "Number of Missing Men of S-51 Definitely Set at 34 by New London," September 25, 1925, 1.

———. "One Killed in Crash of Plane on Ice," February 22, 1982, 1.

———. "Pawtucket Police Force Is Crippled," August 20, 1925, 10.

———. "Pilot Cleared in Woon. Crash," October 8, 1960, 5.

———. "Plane Explodes, Seven Killed," June 6, 1944, 1.

———. "Plane into Dwelling, Child Injured," June 7, 1962.

———. "Planes Ply Grim Hunt for Navy Flier Who Bailed Out Last Night," March 24, 1949.

———. "Planes Search Mid-Bay State for Lost Flier," March 25, 1949.

———. "Poem Inspired Bennington Hero," June 5, 1954, 1.

———. "Position of S-51 on Sea Bottom Found; No Signs of Life," September 25, 1925, 1.

———. "Pothier Urges Thorough Probe of Fatal Locomotive Blast," June 28, 1926, 1.

———. "Raised Submarine S-51 Goes Aground in East River N.Y. While Under Tow for Navy Yard at Brooklyn," July 7, 1926, 1.

———. "Raised U.S. Submarine S-51 On Way to Brooklyn Navy Yard, There to Give Up 20 Dead," July 6, 1926, 1.

———. "Requiem High Mass for S-51 Victims at New London," October 12, 1925, 1.

———. "Rescue Operations on Sunken Submarine S-51 Suspended Because of Rolling Seas," September 30, 1925, 1.

———. "Routine Flight Gives Hill Man First Crash View," December 16, 1958.

———. "Searchers Locate Airplane in Bay," February 13, 1943, 1.

———. "Search for Bodies of 25 Men in Ill Fated Submarine S-51 Will Be Made Tomorrow," July 8, 1926, 1.

———. "State May Ask for Two Indictments," April 26, 1916, 7.

———. "Strict Enforcement of Caution Signal Rules Advocated," April 24, 1916, 3.

———. "3 New Yorkers in Fatal Crash," December 7, 1943, 33.

———. "Train Wreck Death Toll Raised to 4 as Fireman Dies," July 1, 1926, 1.

———. "12 of 18 Bodies of Wreckage of Raised Submarine S-51 at Brooklyn Identified," July 10, 1926, 1.

———. "20 Coffins Arrive at Naval Hospital, Newport," September 30, 1925.

———. "Two Bail Out Safely as AF Jet Crashes in North Smithfield," May 19, 1959.

———. "Two Bodies Recovered by Divers from Sunken U.S. Submarine S-51," September 29, 1925, 1.

———. "Two Bomber Crashes Cost the Lives of 14," September 6, 1951.

———. "Two Men Killed as Plane Crashes Near Landing Field," May 28, 1934.

———. "Two More Bodies Recovered from Sunken Submarine S-51 off Block Island," October 2, 1925, 1.

———. "Two of 17 Patients, Mackinac Blast Victims, Are in Serious Condition," August 26, 1925, 1.

———. "2 TNT Bombs Knocked About in Flattop Blast," June 7, 1954, 4.

———. "U.S. Submarine S-51 Rammed and Sunk off Block Island by Steamer, 34 Men in Vessel, 3 Saved," September 25, 1925, 1.

———. "Vague about Plane Crash," June 9, 1962.

———. "Worst Navy Peace Disaster: Carrier on Way to Quonset," May 26, 1954, 1.

Woonsocket Patriot. "Fatal Railway Wreck at Blackstone Junction," October 11, 1895, 6.

———. "Georgiaville, Drowning Accident," June 27, 1873, 1.

———. "Investigation of the *Metis* Disaster," September 13, 1872, 4.

———. "The Late Steamship Calamity," September 6, 1872, 1.

———. "New Haven and New England," October 11, 1895, 3.

U.S. ARMY CRASH INVESTIGATION REPORTS

43-10-30-6, November 4, 1942.

43-2-11-3, March 29, 1943.

43-2-11-4, March 29, 1943.

43-2-11-5, March 29, 1943.

43-2-11-6, March 29, 1943.

45-11-29-16, November 29, 1944.

U.S. NAVY CRASH REPORT BRIEFS

43-6398, March 30, 1943.

43-6399, March 30, 1943.

43-6410, March 30, 1943.

43-6411, March 30, 1943.

43-6424, April 2, 1943.

43-6425, April 2, 1943.

41-10111, December 5, 1943.

44-11364, January 31, 1944.

44-14865, June 6, 1944.

U.S. AIR FORCE CRASH INVESTIGATION REPORTS

59-5-19-2, May 19, 1959.

National Transportation Safety Board Aircraft Accident Reports

\# NTSB-AAR-82-7, Pilgrim Airlines Flight 458, February 21, 1982–July 20, 1982.

Death Certificates

Rhode Island State Archives.
Town of Putnam, Connecticut, Death Records.
Various Rhode Island city and town halls.

Military Records—National Personnel Records Center

9700 Page Ave., St. Louis, MO.

Websites

Harvey, Alva L., S/Sgt. "World War II Sergeant Pilots." U.S. Air Force Museum. www.nationalmuseum.af.mil.
The Official 325th Fighter Group World War II. "Checkered Clan" Association. www.325thfg.org.
Quonset Air Museum. www.theqam.org.
SS *City of Atlanta*. www.uboat.net.
SS *Washington*. www.greatships.net.
USS *Bennington*. www.ussbennington.org.

Oral Interviews

Lieutenant Robert J. Scearce Jr., USAF Retired, and his wife, Fran Scearce, Portland, OR.
Lawrence Webster, aviation historian and archaeologist, Charlestown, RI.

BOOKS

Cressman, Robert J. *USS Ranger, the Navy's First Flattop from Keel to Mast.* Washington, D.C.: Brassey's Inc., circa 2003.

Pierce, John T., Sr. *Historical Tracts of the Town of Portsmouth, Rhode Island.* Portsmouth, RI: Hamilton Printing Co., circa 1991.

Swanborough, Gordon, and Peter M. Bowers. *United States Navy Aircraft Since 1911.* New York: Funk & Wagnalls, circa 1968.

Thompson, Ellery. *Come Aboard the Draggers.* Stonington, CT: Sea Sketches, 1958.

Wordell, M.T., Lt., USN, and Lt. E.N. Seiler, USNR. *Wildcats over Casablanca.* As told to Keith Ayling. Boston: Little, Brown & Co., circa 1943.

WRITTEN ARTICLES

Klasey, Darrell. "Dr. John McMorris, Fume Pipe Inventor, Dies in Airplane Fall." *California Identification Digest* 6, no. 3 (May/June 2006).

———. "The Iodine/Silver Transfer Method for Recording Latent Fingerprints." *California Identification Digest* 6, no. 2 (March/April 2006).

Leone, Mike, Capt. "Order of Daedalians Recognizes Excellence Once Again." *Flightline Magazine* (Summer 2005), 8.

Poulos, George F. "Fleet Air Wing Seven, Pioneer of Modern Antisubmarine Warfare." N.d.

Proctor, Annie, T/Sgt. "Enlisted Pilots Soaring High from Lower Ranks." *Airman Magazine* (December 1996), 34.

PRESS RELEASES

Press release from Polaris Consulting, Inc., Narragansett, RI. May 21, 1992.

ABOUT THE AUTHOR

Jim Ignasher has been interested in history since his youth, but it is only in recent years that he has begun to write about it. He enjoys searching for long-forgotten stories that other authors may have overlooked, thus hoping to give his readers a new perspective on local history.

He is active with the Historical Society of Smithfield, which operates and maintains the historic Smith-Appleby House Museum, and he occasionally gives talks on Smithfield's history. He is also a member of the New England Antiquities Research Association and Historic New England.

Jim also writes a monthly local history column for *Your Smithfield Magazine*, and in May 2010, he received an award from the Rhode Island Press Association for an article he wrote titled "Rescued from the Attic of Our Lives," which appeared in the magazine's November 2009 edition.

This is his fourth book and his third with The History Press.

Visit us at
www.historypress.net